Memoirs of Casanova Volume VI

Memoirs of Casanova Volume VI

Giacomo Casanova

Memoirs of Casanova Volume VI was first published in 1902.

This edition published by Mint Editions 2021.

ISBN 9781513281889 | E-ISBN 9781513286907

Published by Mint Editions®

minteditionbooks.com

Publishing Director: Jennifer Newens
Design & Production: Rachel Lopez Metzger
Project Manager: Micaela Clark
Translated By: Arthur Machen
Typesetting: Westchester Publishing Services

Contents

I. Leave Bologna a Happy Man—The Captain Parts from Us in Reggio, where I Spend a Delightful Night with Henriette—Our Arrival in Parma—Henriette Resumes the Costume of a Woman; Our Mutual Felicity—I Meet Some Relatives of Mine, but Do not Discover Myself 7

II. I Engage a Box at the Opera, in Spite of Henriette's Reluctance—M. Dubois Pays Us a Visit and Dines with Us; My Darling Plays Him a Trick—Henriette Argues on Happiness—We Call on Dubois, and My Wife Displays Her Marvellous Talent—M. Dutillot The Court gives a Splendid Entertainment in the Ducal Gardens—A Fatal Meeting—I Have an Interview with M. D'Antoine, the Favourite of the Infante of Spain 22

III. Henriette Receives the Visit of M. D'Antoine I Accompany Her as Far as Geneva and Then I Lose Her—I Cross the St. Bernard, and Return to Parma—A Letter from Hensiette—My Despair De La Haye Becomes Attached to Me—Unpleasant Adventure with an Actress and Its Consequences—I Turn a Thorough Bigot—Bavois—I Mystify a Bragging Officer 37

IV. I Receive Good News From Venice, to Which City I Return with De la Haye and Bavois—My Three Friends Give Me a Warm Welcome; Their Surprise at Finding Me a Model of Devotion—Bavois Lures Me Back to My Former Way of Living—De la Haye a Thorough Hypocrite—Adventure with the Girl Marchetti—I Win a Prize in the Lottery—I Meet Baletti—De la Haye Leaves M. de Bragadin's Palace—My Departure for Paris 54

V. I Stop at Ferrara, Where I Have a Comic Adventure—My Arrival in Paris 68

| VI. | My Apprenticeship in Paris—Portraits—Oddities—All Sorts of Things | 81 |

| VII. | My Blunders in the French Language, My Success, My Numerous Acquaintances—Louis XV—My Brother Arrives in Paris | 100 |

| VIII. | My Broil with Parisian Justice—Mdlle. Vesian | 119 |

| IX. | The Beautiful O-Morphi—The Deceitful Painter—I Practice Cabalism for the Duchess de Chartres I Leave Paris—My Stay in Dresden and My Departure from that City | 138 |

I

Leave Bologna a Happy Man—The Captain Parts from Us in Reggio, where I Spend a Delightful Night with Henriette—Our Arrival in Parma—Henriette Resumes the Costume of a Woman; Our Mutual Felicity—I Meet Some Relatives of Mine, but Do not Discover Myself.

The reader can easily guess that there was a change as sudden as a transformation in a pantomime, and that the short but magic sentence, "Come to Parma," proved a very fortunate catastrophe, thanks to which I rapidly changed, passing from the tragic to the gentle mood, from the serious to the tender tone. Sooth to say, I fell at her feet, and lovingly pressing her knees I kissed them repeatedly with raptures of gratitude. No more 'furore', no more bitter words; they do not suit the sweetest of all human feelings! Loving, docile, grateful, I swear never to beg for any favour, not even to kiss her hand, until I have shewn myself worthy of her precious love! The heavenly creature, delighted to see me pass so rapidly from despair to the most lively tenderness, tells me, with a voice the tone of which breathes of love, to get up from my knees.

"I am sure that you love me," says she, "and be quite certain that I shall leave nothing undone to secure the constancy of your feelings." Even if she had said that she loved me as much as I adored her, she would not have been more eloquent, for her words expressed all that can be felt. My lips were pressed to her beautiful hands as the captain entered the room. He complimented us with perfect good faith, and I told him, my face beaming with happiness, that I was going to order the carriage. I left them together, and in a short time we were on our road, cheerful, pleased, and merry.

Before reaching Reggio the honest captain told me that in his opinion it would be better for him to proceed to Parma alone, as, if we arrived in that city all together, it might cause some remarks, and people would talk about us much less if we were without him. We both thought him quite right, and we immediately made up our minds to pass the night in Reggio, while the captain would take a post-chaise and go alone to Parma. According to that arrangement his trunk was transferred to the vehicle which he hired in Reggio, he bade us farewell and went away, after having promised to dine with us on the following day in Parma.

The decision taken by the worthy Hungarian was, doubtless, as agreeable to my lovely friend as to me, for our delicacy would have condemned us to a great reserve in his presence. And truly, under the new circumstances, how were we to arrange for our lodgings in Reggio? Henriette could not, of course, share the bed of the captain any more, and she could not have slept with me as long as he was with us, without being guilty of great immodesty. We should all three have laughed at that compulsory reserve which we would have felt to be ridiculous, but we should, for all that, have submitted to it. Love is the little impudent god, the enemy of bashfulness, although he may very often enjoy darkness and mystery, but if he gives way to it he feels disgraced; he loses three-fourths of his dignity and the greatest portion of his charms.

Evidently there could be no happiness for Henriette or for me unless we parted with the person and even with the remembrance of the excellent captain.

We supped alone. I was intoxicated with a felicity which seemed too immense, and yet I felt melancholy, but Henriette, who looked sad likewise, had no reproach to address to me. Our sadness was in reality nothing but shyness; we loved each other, but we had had no time to become acquainted. We exchanged only a few words, there was nothing witty, nothing interesting in our conversation, which struck us both as insipid, and we found more pleasure in the thoughts which filled our minds. We knew that we were going to pass the night together, but we could not have spoken of it openly. What a night! what a delightful creature was that Henriette whom I have loved so deeply, who has made me so supremely happy!

It was only three or four days later that I ventured on asking her what she would have done, without a groat in her possession, having not one acquaintance in Parma, if I had been afraid to declare my love, and if I had gone to Naples. She answered that she would doubtless have found herself in very great difficulties, but that she had all along felt certain of my love, and that she had foreseen what had happened. She added that, being impatient to know what I thought of her, she had asked me to translate to the captain what she had expressed respecting her resolution, knowing that he could neither oppose that resolution nor continue to live with her, and that, as she had taken care not to include me in the prayer which she had addressed to him through me, she had thought it impossible that I should fail to ask whether I could be of some service to her, waiting to take a decision until she could have ascertained the nature of my feelings towards her. She concluded by telling me that if she had fallen it was the fault of her husband and of her father-in-law, both of whom she characterized as monsters rather than men.

When we reached Parma, I gave the police the name of Farusi, the same that I had assumed in Cesena; it was the family name of my mother; while Henriette wrote down, "Anne D'Arci, from France." While we were answering the questions of the officer, a young Frenchman, smart and intelligent-looking, offered me his services, and advised me not to put up at the posting-inn, but to take lodgings at D'Andremorit's hotel, where I should find good apartments, French cooking, and the best French wines.

Seeing that Henriette was pleased with the proposal, I told the young man to take us there, and we were soon very comfortably lodged. I engaged the Frenchman by the day, and carefully settled all my arrangements with D'Andremont. After that I attended to the housing of my carriage.

Coming in again for a few minutes, I told Henriette that I would return in time for dinner, and, ordering the servant to remain in the ante-room, I went out alone.

Parma was then groaning under a new government. I had every reason to suppose that there were spies everywhere and under every form. I therefore did not want to have at my heels a valet who might have injured rather than served me. Though I was in my father's native city, I had no acquaintances there, but I knew that I should soon find my way.

When I found myself in the streets, I scarcely could believe that I was in Italy, for everything had a tramontane appearance. I heard nothing but French and Spanish, and those who did not speak one of those languages seemed to be whispering to one another. I was going about at random, looking for a hosier, yet unwilling to enquire where I could find one; at last I saw what I wanted.

I entered the shop, and addressing myself to a stout, good-looking woman seated behind the counter, I said,

"Madam, I wish to make some purchases."

"Sir, shall I send for someone speaking French?"

"You need not do so, I am an Italian."

"God be praised! Italians are scarce in these days."

"Why scarce?"

"Do you not know that Don Philip has arrived, and that his wife, Madame de France, is on the road?"

"I congratulate you, for it must make trade very good. I suppose that money is plentiful, and that there is abundance of all commodities."

"That is true, but everything is high in price, and we cannot get reconciled to these new fashions. They are a bad mixture of French freedom and Spanish haughtiness which addles our brains. But, sir, what sort of linen do you require?"

"In the first place, I must tell you that I never try to drive a hard bargain, therefore be careful. If you charge me too much, I shall not come again. I want some fine linen for twenty-four chemises, some dimity for stays and petticoats, some muslin, some cambric for pocket-handkerchiefs, and many other articles which I should be very glad to find in your shop, for I am a stranger here, and God knows in what hands I am going to trust myself!"

"You will be in honest ones, if you will give me your confidence."

"I am sure that you deserve it, and I abandon my interests to you. I want likewise to find some needlewomen willing to work in the lady's room, because she requires everything to be made very rapidly."

"And dresses?"

"Yes, dresses, caps, mantles-in fact, everything, for she is naked."

"With money she will soon have all she wants. Is she young?"

"She is four years younger than I. She is my wife."

"Ah! may God bless you! Any children?"

"Not yet, my good lady; but they will come, for we do all that is necessary to have them."

"I have no doubt of it. How pleased I am! Well, sir, I shall send for the very phoenix of all dressmakers. In the mean time, choose what you require, it will amuse you."

I took the best of everything and paid, and the dressmaker making her appearance at that moment I gave my address, requesting that various sorts of stuff might be sent at once. I told the dressmaker and her daughter, who had come with her, to follow me and to carry the linen. On my way to the hotel I bought several pairs of silk stockings, and took with me a bootmaker who lived close by.

Oh, what a delightful moment! Henriette, who had not the slightest idea of what I had gone out for, looked at everything with great pleasure, yet without any of those demonstrations which announce a selfish or interested disposition. She shewed her gratitude only by the delicate praise which she bestowed upon my taste and upon the quality of the articles I had purchased. She was not more cheerful on account of my presents, but the tender affection with which she looked at me was the best proof of her grateful feelings.

The valet I had hired had entered the room with the shoemaker. Henriette told him quietly to withdraw, and not to come unless he was called. The dressmaker set to work, the shoemaker took her measure, and I told him to bring some slippers. He returned in a short time, and the valet came in again with him without having been called. The shoemaker, who spoke French, was talking the usual nonsense of dealers, when she interrupted him to ask the valet, who was standing familiarly in the room, what he wanted.

"Nothing, madam, I am only waiting for your orders."

"Have I not told you that you would be called when your services were required?"

"I should like to know who is my master, you or the gentleman?"

"Neither," I replied, laughing. "Here are your day's wages. Be off at once."

The shoemaker, seeing that Henriette spoke only French, begged to recommend a teacher of languages.

"What country does he belong to?" she enquired.

"To Flanders, madam," answered Crispin, "he is a very learned man, about fifty years old. He is said to be a good man. He charges three libbre for each lesson of one hour, and six for two hours, but he requires to be paid each time."

"My dear," said Henriette to me, "do you wish me to engage that master?"

"Yes, dearest, it will amuse you."

The shoemaker promised to send the Flemish professor the next morning.

The dressmakers were hard at work, the mother cutting and the daughter sewing, but, as progress could not be too rapid, I told the mother that she would oblige us if she could procure another seamstress who spoke French.

"You shall have one this very day, sir," she answered, and she offered me the services of her own son as a servant, saying that if I took him I should be certain to have neither a thief nor a spy about me, and that he spoke French pretty well. Henriette thought we could not do better than take the young man. Of course that was enough to make me consent at once, for the slightest wish of the woman we love is our supreme law. The mother went for him, and she brought back at the same time the half-French dressmaker. It all amused my goddess, who looked very happy.

The young man was about eighteen, pleasant, gentle and modest. I enquired his name, and he answered that it was Caudagna.

The reader may very likely recollect that my father's native place had been Parma, and that one of his sisters had married a Caudagna. "It would be a curious coincidence," I thought, "if that dressmaker should be my aunt, and my valet my cousin!" but I did not say it aloud.

Henriette asked me if I had any objection to the first dressmaker dining at our table.

"I entreat you, my darling," I answered, "never, for the future, to ask my consent in such trifling matters. Be quite certain, my beloved, that I shall always approve everything you may do."

She smiled and thanked me. I took out my purse, and said to her;

"Take these fifty sequins, dearest, to pay for all your small expenses, and to buy the many trifles which I should be sure to forget."

She took the money, assuring me that she was vastly obliged to me.

A short time before dinner the worthy captain made his appearance. Henriette ran to meet him and kissed him, calling him her dear father, and I followed her example by calling him my friend. My beloved little wife invited him to dine with us every day. The excellent fellow, seeing all the women working busily for Henriette, was highly pleased at having procured such a good position for his young adventuress, and I crowned his happiness by telling him that I was indebted to him for my felicity.

Our dinner was delicious, and it proved a cheerful meal. I found out that Henriette was dainty, and my old friend a lover of good wines. I was both, and felt that I was a match for them. We tasted several excellent wines which D'Andremont had recommended, and altogether we had a very good dinner.

The young valet pleased me in consequence of the respectful manner in which he served everyone, his mother as well as his masters. His sister and the other seamstress had dined apart.

We were enjoying our dessert when the hosier was announced, accompanied by another woman and a milliner who could speak

French. The other woman had brought patterns of all sorts of dresses. I let Henriette order caps, head-dresses, etc., as she pleased, but I would interfere in the dress department although I complied with the excellent taste of my charming friend. I made her choose four dresses, and I was indeed grateful for her ready acceptance of them, for my own happiness was increased in proportion to the pleasure I gave her and the influence I was obtaining over her heart.

Thus did we spend the first day, and we could certainly not have accomplished more.

In the evening, as we were alone at supper, I fancied that her lovely face looked sad. I told her so.

"My darling," she answered, with a voice which went to my heart, "you are spending a great deal of money on me, and if you do so in the hope of my loving you more dearly I must tell you it is money lost, for I do not love you now more than I did yesterday, but I do love you with my whole heart. All you may do that is not strictly necessary pleases me only because I see more and more how worthy you are of me, but it is not needed to make me feel all the deep love which you deserve."

"I believe you, dearest, and my happiness is indeed great if you feel that your love for me cannot be increased. But learn also, delight of my heart, that I have done it all only to try to love you even more than I do, if possible. I wish to see you beautiful and brilliant in the attire of your sex, and if there is one drop of bitterness in the fragrant cup of my felicity, it is a regret at not being able to surround you with the halo which you deserve. Can I be otherwise than delighted, my love, if you are pleased?"

"You cannot for one moment doubt my being pleased, and as you have called me your wife you are right in one way, but if you are not very rich I leave it to you to judge how deeply I ought to reproach myself."

"Ah, my beloved angel! let me, I beg of you, believe myself wealthy, and be quite certain that you cannot possibly be the cause of my ruin. You were born only for my happiness. All I wish is that you may never leave me. Tell me whether I can entertain such a hope."

"I wish it myself, dearest, but who can be sure of the future? Are you free? Are you dependent on anyone?"

"I am free in the broadest meaning of that word, I am dependent on no one but you, and I love to be so."

"I congratulate you, and I am very glad of it, for no one can tear you from my arms, but, alas! you know that I cannot say the same as you. I am certain that some persons are, even now, seeking for me, and they will not find it very difficult to secure me if they ever discover where I am. Alas! I feel how miserable I should be if they ever succeeded in dragging me away from you!"

"You make me tremble. Are you afraid of such a dreadful misfortune here?"

"No, unless I should happen to be seen by someone knowing me."

"Are any such persons likely to be here at present?"

"I think not."

"Then do not let our love take alarm, I trust your fears will never be verified. Only, my darling one, you must be as cheerful as you were in Cesena."

"I shall be more truly so now, dear friend. In Cesena I was miserable; while now I am happy. Do not be afraid of my being sad, for I am of a naturally cheerful disposition."

"I suppose that in Cesena you were afraid of being caught by the officer whom you had left in Rome?"

"Not at all; that officer was my father-in-law, and I am quite certain that he never tried to ascertain where I had gone. He was only too glad to get rid of me. I felt unhappy because I could not bear to be a charge on a man whom I could not love, and with whom I could not even exchange one thought. Recollect also that I could not find consolation in the idea that I was ministering to his happiness, for I had only inspired him with a passing fancy which he had himself valued at ten sequins. I could not help feeling that his fancy, once gratified, was not likely at his time of life to become a more lasting sentiment, and I could therefore only be a burden to him, for he was not wealthy. Besides, there was a miserable consideration which increased my secret sorrow. I thought myself bound in duty to caress him, and on his side, as he thought that he ought to pay me in the same money, I was afraid of his ruining his health for me, and that idea made me very unhappy. Having no love for each other, we allowed a foolish feeling of regard to make both of us uncomfortable. We lavished, for the sake of a well-meaning but false decorum, that which belongs to love alone. Another thing troubled me greatly. I was afraid lest people might suppose that I was a source of profit to him. That idea made me feel the deepest shame, yet, whenever I thought of it, I could not help admitting that such a supposition, however false, was not wanting in probability. It is owing to that feeling that you found me so reserved towards you, for I was afraid that you might harbour that fearful idea if I allowed, you to read in my looks the favourable impression which you had made on my heart."

"Then it was not owing to a feeling of self-love?"

"No, I confess it, for you could but judge me as I deserved. I had been guilty of the folly now known to you because my father-in-law intended to bury me in a convent, and that did not suit my taste. But, dearest friend, you must forgive me if, I cannot confide even to you the history of my life."

"I respect your secret, darling; you need not fear any intrusion from me on that subject. All we have to do is to love one another, and not to allow any dread of the future to mar our actual felicity."

The next day, after a night of intense enjoyment, I found myself more deeply in love than before, and the next three months were spent by us in an intoxication of delight.

At nine o'clock the next morning the teacher of Italian was announced. I saw a man of respectable appearance, polite, modest, speaking little but well, reserved in his answers, and with the manners of olden times. We conversed, and I could not help laughing when he said, with an air of perfect good faith, that a Christian could only admit the system of Copernicus as a clever hypothesis. I answered that it was the system of God Himself because it was that of nature, and that it was not in Holy Scripture that the laws of science could be learned.

The teacher smiled in a manner which betrayed the Tartufe, and if I had consulted only my own feelings I should have dismissed the poor man, but I thought that he might amuse Henriette and teach her Italian; after all it was what I wanted from him. My dear wife told him that she would give him six libbre for a lesson of two hours: the libbra of Parma being worth only about threepence, his lessons were not very expensive. She took her first lesson immediately and gave him two sequins, asking him to purchase her some good novels.

Whilst my dear Henriette was taking her lesson, I had some conversation with the dressmaker, in order to ascertain whether she was a relative of mine.

"What does your husband do?" I asked her.

"He is steward to the Marquis of Sissa."

"Is your father still alive?"

"No, sir, he is dead."

"What was his family name?"

"Scotti."

"Are your husband's parents still alive?"

"His father is dead, but his mother is still alive, and resides with her uncle, Canon Casanova."

That was enough. The good woman was my Welsh cousin, and her children were my Welsh nephews. My niece Jeanneton was not pretty; but she appeared to be a good girl. I continued my conversation with the mother, but I changed the topic.

"Are the Parmesans satisfied with being the subjects of a Spanish prince?"

"Satisfied? Well, in that case, we should be easily pleased, for we are now in a regular maze. Everything is upset, we do not know where we are. Oh! happy times of the house of Farnese, whither have you departed? The day before yesterday I went to the theatre, and Harlequin made everybody roar with laughter. Well, now, fancy, Don Philipo, our new duke, did all he could to remain serious, and when he could not manage it, he would hide his face in his hat so that people should not see that he was laughing, for it is said that laughter ought never to disturb the grave and stiff countenance of an Infante of Spain, and that he would be dishonoured in Madrid if he did not conceal his mirth. What do you think of that? Can such manners suit us? Here we laugh willingly and heartily! Oh! the good Duke Antonio (God rest his soul!) was certainly as great a prince as Duke Philipo, but he did not hide himself from his subjects when he was pleased, and he would sometimes laugh so heartily that he could be heard in the streets. Now we are all in the most fearful confusion, and for the last three months no one in Parma knows what's o'clock."

"Have all the clocks been destroyed?"

"No, but ever since God created the world, the sun has always gone down at half-past five, and at six the bells have always been tolled for the Angelus. All respectable people knew that at that time the candle had to be lit. Now, it is very strange, the sun has gone mad, for he sets every day at a different hour. Our peasants do not know when they are to come to market. All that is called a regulation but do you know why? Because now everybody knows that dinner is to be eaten at twelve o'clock. A fine regulation, indeed! Under the Farnese we used to eat when we were hungry, and that was much better."

That way of reasoning was certainly singular, but I did not think it sounded foolish in the mouth of a woman of humble rank. It seems to me that a government ought never to destroy ancient customs abruptly, and that innocent errors ought to be corrected only by degrees.

Henriette had no watch. I felt delighted at the idea of offering her such a present, and I went out to purchase one, but after I had bought a very fine watch, I thought of ear-rings, of a fan, and of many other pretty nicknacks. Of course I bought them all at once. She received all those gifts offered by love with a tender delicacy which overjoyed me. She was still with the teacher when I came back.

"I should have been able," he said to me, "to teach your lady heraldry, geography, history, and the use of the globes, but she knows that already. She has received an excellent education."

The teacher's name was Valentin de la Haye. He told me that he was an engineer and professor of mathematics. I shall have to speak of him very often in these Memoirs, and my readers will make his acquaintance by his deeds better than by any portrait I could give of him, so I will merely say that he was a true Tartufe, a worthy pupil of Escobar.

We had a pleasant dinner with our Hungarian friend. Henriette was still wearing the uniform, and I longed to see her dressed as a woman. She expected a dress to be ready for the next day, and she was already supplied with petticoats and chemises.

Henriette was full of wit and a mistress of repartee. The milliner, who was a native of Lyons, came in one morning, and said in French:

"Madame et Monsieur, j'ai l'honneur de vous souhaiter le bonjour."

"Why," said my friend, "do you not say Monsieur et madame?"

"I have always heard that in society the precedence is given to the ladies."

"But from whom do we wish to receive that honour?"

"From gentlemen, of course."

"And do you not see that women would render themselves ridiculous if they did not grant to men the same that they expect from them. If we wish them never to fail in politeness towards us, we must shew them the example."

"Madam," answered the shrewd milliner, "you have taught me an excellent lesson, and I will profit by it. Monsieur et madame, je suis votre servante."

This feminine controversy greatly amused me.

Those who do not believe that a woman can make a man happy through the twenty-four hours of the day have never possessed a woman like Henriette. The happiness which filled me, if I can express it in that manner, was much greater when I conversed with her even than when I held her in my arms. She had read much, she had great tact, and her taste was naturally excellent; her judgment was sane, and, without being learned, she could argue like a mathematician, easily and without pretension, and in everything she had that natural grace which is so charming. She never tried to be witty when she said something of importance, but accompanied her words with a smile which imparted to them an appearance of trifling, and brought them within the understanding of all. In that way she would give intelligence even to those who had none, and she won every heart. Beauty without wit offers love nothing but the material enjoyment of its physical charms, whilst witty ugliness captivates by the charms of the mind, and at last fulfils all the desires of the man it has captivated.

Then what was my position during all the time that I possessed my beautiful and witty Henriette? That of a man so supremely happy that I could scarcely realize my felicity!

Let anyone ask a beautiful woman without wit whether she would be willing to exchange a small portion of her beauty for a sufficient dose of wit. If she speaks the truth, she will say, "No, I am satisfied to be as I am." But why is she satisfied? Because she is not aware of her own deficiency. Let an ugly but witty woman be asked if she would change her wit against beauty, and she will not hesitate in saying no. Why? Because, knowing the value of her wit, she is well aware that it is sufficient by itself to make her a queen in any society.

But a learned woman, a blue-stocking, is not the creature to minister to a man's happiness. Positive knowledge is not a woman's province. It is antipathetic to the gentleness of her nature, to the amenity, to the sweet timidity which are the greatest charms of the fair sex, besides, women never carry their learning beyond certain limits, and the tittle-tattle of blue-stockings can dazzle no one but fools. There has never been one great discovery due to a woman. The fair sex is deficient in that vigorous power which the body lends to the mind, but women are evidently superior to men in simple reasoning, in delicacy of feelings, and in that species of merit which appertains to the heart rather than to the mind.

Hurl some idle sophism at a woman of intelligence. She will not unravel it, but she will not be deceived by it, and, though she may not say so, she will let you guess that she does not accept it. A man, on the contrary, if he cannot unravel the sophism, takes it in a literal sense, and in that respect the learned woman is exactly the same as man. What a burden a Madame Dacier must be to a man! May God save every honest man from such!

When the new dress was brought, Henriette told me that she did not want me to witness the process of her metamorphosis, and she desired me to go out for a walk until she had resumed her original form. I obeyed cheerfully, for the slightest wish of the woman we love is a law, and our very obedience increases our happiness.

As I had nothing particular to do, I went to a French bookseller in whose shop I made the acquaintance of a witty hunchback, and I must say that a hunchback without wit is a raga avis; I have found it so in all countries. Of course it is not wit which gives the hump, for, thank God, all witty men are not humpbacked, but we may well say that as a general rule the hump gives wit, for the very small number of hunchbacks who have little or no wit only confirms the rule: The one I was alluding to just now was called Dubois-Chateleraux. He was a skilful engraver, and director of the Mint of Parma for the Infante, although that prince could not boast of such an institution.

I spent an hour with the witty hunchback, who shewed me several of his engravings, and I returned to the hotel where I found the Hungarian waiting to see Henriette. He did not know that she would that morning receive us in the attire of her sex. The door was thrown open, and a beautiful, charming woman met us with a courtesy full of grace, which no longer reminded us of the stiffness or of the too great freedom which belong to the military costume. Her sudden appearance certainly astonished us, and we did not know what to say or what to do. She invited us to be seated, looked at the captain in a friendly manner, and pressed my hand with the warmest affection, but without giving way any more to that outward familiarity which a young officer can assume, but which does not suit a well-educated lady. Her noble and modest bearing soon compelled me to put myself in unison with her, and I did so without difficulty, for she was not acting a part, and the way in which she had resumed her natural character made it easy for me to follow her on that ground.

I was gazing at her with admiration, and, urged by a feeling which I did not take time to analyze, I took her hand to kiss it with respect, but, without giving me an opportunity of raising it to my lips, she offered me her lovely mouth. Never did a kiss taste so delicious.

"Am I not then always the same?" said she to me, with deep feeling.

"No, heavenly creature, and it is so true that you are no longer the same in my eyes that I could not now use any familiarity towards you. You are no longer the witty, free young officer who told Madame Querini about the game of Pharaoh, end about the deposits made to your bank by the captain in so niggardly a manner that they were hardly worth mentioning."

"It is very true that, wearing the costume of my sex, I should never dare to utter such words. Yet, dearest friend, it does not prevent my being your Henriette—that Henriette who has in her life been guilty of three escapades, the last of which would have utterly ruined me if it had not been for you, but which I call a delightful error, since it has been the cause of my knowing you."

Those words moved me so deeply that I was on the point of throwing myself at her feet, to entreat her to forgive me for not having shewn her more respect, but Henriette, who saw the state in which I was, and who wanted to put an end to the pathetic scene, began to shake our poor captain, who sat as motionless as a statue, and as if he had been petrified. He felt ashamed at having treated such a woman as an adventuress, for he knew that what he now saw was not an illusion. He kept looking at her with great confusion, and bowing most respectfully, as if he wanted to atone for his past conduct towards her. As for Henriette, she seemed to say to him, but without the shadow of a reproach;

"I am glad that you think me worth more than ten sequins."

We sat down to dinner, and from that moment she did the honours of the table with the perfect ease of a person who is accustomed to fulfil that difficult duty. She treated me like a beloved husband, and the captain like a respected friend. The poor Hungarian begged me to tell her that if he had seen her, as she was now, in Civita Vecchia, when she came out of the tartan, he should never have dreamed of dispatching his cicerone to her room.

"Oh! tell him that I do not doubt it. But is it not strange that a poor little female dress should command more respect than the garb of an officer?"

"Pray do not abuse the officer's costume, for it is to it that I am indebted for my happiness."

"Yes," she said, with a loving smile, "as I owe mine to the sbirri of Cesena."

We remained for a long time at the table, and our delightful conversation turned upon no other topic than our mutual felicity. If it had not been for the uneasiness of the poor captain, which at last struck us, we should never have put a stop either to the dinner or to, our charming prattle.

II

I Engage a Box at the Opera, in Spite of Henriette's Reluctance—M. Dubois Pays Us a Visit and Dines with Us; My Darling Plays Him a Trick—Henriette Argues on Happiness—We Call on Dubois, and My Wife Displays Her Marvellous Talent—M. Dutillot The Court gives a Splendid Entertainment in the Ducal Gardens—A Fatal Meeting—I Have an Interview with M. D'Antoine, the Favourite of the Infante of Spain.

The happiness I was enjoying was too complete to last long. I was fated to lose it, but I must not anticipate events. Madame de France, wife of the Infante Don Philip, having arrived in Parma, the opera house was opened, and I engaged a private box, telling Henriette that I intended to take her to the theatre every night. She had several times confessed that she had a great passion for music, and I had no doubt that she would be pleased with my proposal. She had never yet seen an Italian opera, and I felt certain that she wished to ascertain whether the Italian music deserved its universal fame. But I was indeed surprised when she exclaimed,

"What, dearest! You wish to go every evening to the opera?"

"I think, my love, that, if we did not go, we should give some excuse for scandal-mongers to gossip. Yet, should you not like it, you know that there is no need for us to go. Do not think of me, for I prefer our pleasant chat in this room to the heavenly concert of the seraphs."

"I am passionately fond of music, darling, but I cannot help trembling at the idea of going out."

"If you tremble, I must shudder, but we ought to go to the opera or leave Parma. Let us go to London or to any other place. Give your orders, I am ready to do anything you like."

"Well, take a private box as little exposed as possible."

"How kind you are!"

The box I had engaged was in the second tier, but the theatre being small it was difficult for a pretty woman to escape observation.

I told her so.

"I do not think there is any danger," she answered; "for I have not seen the name of any person of my acquaintance in the list of foreigners which you gave me to read."

Thus did Henriette go to the opera. I had taken care that our box should not be lighted up. It was an opera-buffa, the music of Burellano was excellent, and the singers were very good.

Henriette made no use of her opera-glass except to look on the stage, and nobody paid any attention to us. As she had been greatly pleased with the finale of the second act, I promised to get it for her, and I asked Dubois to procure it for me. Thinking that she could play the harpsichord, I offered to get one, but she told me that she had never touched that instrument.

On the night of the fourth or fifth performance M. Dubois came to our box, and as I did not wish to introduce him to my friend, I only asked what I could do for him. He then handed me the music I had begged him to purchase for me, and I paid him what it had cost, offering him my best thanks. As we were just opposite the ducal box, I asked him, for the sake of saying something, whether he had engraved the portraits of their highnesses. He answered that he had already engraved two medals, and I gave him an order for both, in gold. He promised to let me have them, and left the box. Henriette had not even looked at him, and that was according to all established rules, as I had not introduced him, but the next morning he was announced as we were at dinner. M. de la Haye, who was dining with us, complimented us upon having made the acquaintance of Dubois, and introduced him to his pupil the moment he came into the room. It was then right for Henriette to welcome him, which she did most gracefully.

After she had thanked him for the 'partizione', she begged he would get her some other music, and the artist accepted her request as a favour granted to him.

"Sir," said Dubois to me, "I have taken the liberty of bringing the medals you wished to have; here they are."

On one were the portraits of the Infante and his wife, on the other was engraved only the head of Don Philip. They were both beautifully engraved, and we expressed our just admiration. "The workmanship is beyond all price," said Henriette, "but the gold can be bartered for other gold." "Madam," answered the modest artist, "the medals weight sixteen sequins." She gave him the amount immediately, and invited him to call again at dinner-time. Coffee was just brought in at that moment, and she asked him to take it with us. Before sweetening his cup, she enquired whether he liked his coffee very sweet.

"Your taste, madam," answered the hunchback, gallantly, "is sure to be mine."

"Then you have guessed that I always drink coffee without sugar. I am glad we have that taste in common."

And she gracefully offered him the cup of coffee without sugar. She then helped De la Haye and me, not forgetting to put plenty of sugar in our cups, and she poured out one for herself exactly like the one she handed to Dubois. It was much ado for me not to laugh, for my mischievous French-woman, who liked her coffee in the Parisian fashion, that is to say very sweet, was sipping the bitter beverage with an air of delight which compelled the director of the Mint to smile under the infliction. But the cunning hunchback was even with her; accepting the penalty of his foolish compliment, and praising the good quality of the coffee, he boldly declared that it was the only way to taste the delicious aroma of the precious berry.

When Dubois and De la Haye had left us, we both laughed at the trick.

"But," said I to Henriette, "you will be the first victim of your mischief, for whenever he dines with us, you must keep up the joke, in order not to betray yourself."

"Oh! I can easily contrive to drink my coffee well sweetened, and to make him drain the bitter cup."

At the end of one month, Henriette could speak Italian fluently, and it was owing more to the constant practice she had every day with my cousin Jeanneton, who acted as her maid, than to the lessons of Professor de la Haye. The lessons only taught her the rules, and practice is necessary to acquire a language. I have experienced it myself. I learned more French during the too short period that I spent so happily with my charming Henriette than in all the lessons I had taken from Dalacqua.

We had attended the opera twenty times without making any acquaintance, and our life was indeed supremely happy. I never went out without Henriette, and always in a carriage; we never received anyone, and nobody knew us. Dubois was the only person, since the departure of the good Hungarian, who sometimes dined with us; I do not reckon De la Haye, who was a daily guest at our table. Dubois felt great curiosity about us, but he was cunning and did not shew his curiosity; we were reserved without affectation, and his inquisitiveness was at fault. One day he mentioned to us that the court of the Infante of Parma was very brilliant since the arrival of Madame de France, and that there were many foreigners of both sexes in the city. Then, turning towards Henriette, he said to her;

"Most of the foreign ladies whom we have here are unknown to us."

"Very likely, many of them would not shew themselves if they were known."

"Very likely, madam, as you say, but I can assure you that, even if their beauty and the richness of their toilet made them conspicuous, our sovereigns wish for freedom. I still hope, madam, that we shall have the happiness of seeing you at the court of the duke."

"I do not think so, for, in my opinion, it is superlatively ridiculous for a lady to go to the court without being presented, particularly if she has a right to be so."

The last words, on which Henriette had laid a little more stress than upon the first part of her answer, struck our little hunchback dumb, and my friend, improving her opportunity, changed the subject of conversation.

When he had gone we enjoyed the check she had thus given to the inquisitiveness of our guest, but I told Henriette that, in good conscience, she ought to forgive all those whom she rendered curious, because... she cut my words short by covering me with loving kisses.

Thus supremely happy, and finding in one another constant satisfaction, we would laugh at those morose philosophers who deny that complete happiness can be found on earth.

"What do they mean, darling—those crazy fools—by saying that happiness is not lasting, and how do they understand that word? If they mean everlasting, immortal, unintermitting, of course they are right, but the life of man not being such, happiness, as a natural consequence, cannot be such either. Otherwise, every happiness is lasting for the very reason that it does exist, and to be lasting it requires only to exist. But if by complete felicity they understand a series of varied and never-interrupted pleasures, they are wrong, because, by allowing after each pleasure the calm which ought to follow the enjoyment of it, we have time to realize happiness in its reality. In other words those necessary periods of repose are a source of true enjoyment, because, thanks to them, we enjoy the delight of recollection which increases twofold the reality of happiness. Man can be happy only when in his own mind he realizes his happiness, and calm is necessary to give full play to his mind; therefore without calm man would truly never be completely happy, and pleasure, in order to be felt, must cease to be active. Then what do they mean by that word lasting?

"Every day we reach a moment when we long for sleep, and, although it be the very likeness of non-existence, can anyone deny that sleep is a pleasure? No, at least it seems to me that it cannot be denied with consistency, for, the moment it comes to us, we give it the preference over all other pleasures, and we are grateful to it only after it has left us.

"Those who say that no one can be happy throughout life speak likewise frivolously. Philosophy teaches the secret of securing that happiness, provided one is free from bodily sufferings. A felicity which would thus last throughout life could be compared to a nosegay formed of a thousand flowers so beautifully, so skillfully blended together, that it would look one single flower. Why should it be impossible for us to spend here the whole of our life as we have spent the last month, always in good health, always loving one another, without ever feeling any other want or any weariness? Then, to crown that happiness, which would certainly be immense, all that would be wanted would be to die together, in an advanced age, speaking to the last moment of our pleasant recollections. Surely that felicity would have been lasting. Death would not interrupt it, for death would end it. We could not, even then, suppose ourselves unhappy unless we dreaded unhappiness after death, and such an idea strikes me as absurd, for it is a contradiction of the idea of an almighty and fatherly tenderness."

It was thus that my beloved Henriette would often make me spend delightful hours, talking philosophic sentiment. Her logic was better than that of Cicero in his Tusculan Disputations, but she admitted that such lasting felicity could exist only between two beings who lived together, and loved each other with constant affection, healthy in mind and in body, enlightened, sufficiently rich, similar in tastes, in disposition, and in temperament. Happy are those lovers who, when their senses require rest, can fall back upon the intellectual enjoyments afforded by the mind! Sweet sleep then comes, and lasts until the body has recovered its general harmony. On awaking, the senses are again active and always ready to resume their action.

The conditions of existence are exactly the same for man as for the universe, I might almost say that between them there is perfect identity, for if we take the universe away, mankind no longer exists, and if we take mankind away, there is no longer an universe; who could realize the idea of the existence of inorganic matter? Now, without that idea, 'nihil est', since the idea is the essence of everything, and since man alone has ideas. Besides, if we abstract the species, we can no longer imagine the existence of matter, and vice versa.

I derived from Henriette as great happiness as that charming woman derived from me. We loved one another with all the strength of our faculties, and we were everything to each other. She would often repeat those pretty lines of the good La, Fontaine:

> *'Soyez-vous l'un a l'autre un monde toujours beau,*
> *Toujours divers, toujours nouveau;*
> *Tenez-vous lieu de tout; comptez pour rien le reste.'*

And we did not fail to put the advice into practice, for never did a minute of ennui or of weariness, never did the slightest trouble, disturb our bliss.

The day after the close of the opera, Dubois, who was dining with us, said that on the following day he was entertaining the two first artists, 'primo cantatore' and 'prima cantatrice', and added that, if we liked to come, we would hear some of their best pieces, which they were to sing in a lofty hall of his country-house particularly adapted to the display of the human voice. Henriette thanked him warmly, but she said that, her health being very delicate, she could not engage herself beforehand, and she spoke of other things.

When we were alone, I asked her why she had refused the pleasure offered by Dubois.

"I should accept his invitation," she answered, "and with delight, if I were not afraid of meeting at his house some person who might know me, and would destroy the happiness I am now enjoying with you."

"If you have any fresh motive for dreading such an occurrence, you are quite right, but if it is only a vague, groundless fear, my love, why should you deprive yourself of a real and innocent pleasure? If you knew how pleased I am when I see you enjoy yourself, and particularly when I witness your ecstacy in listening to fine music!"

"Well, darling, I do not want to shew myself less brave than you. We will go immediately after dinner. The artists will not sing before. Besides, as he does not expect us, he is not likely to have invited any person curious to speak to me. We will go without giving him notice of our coming, without being expected, and as if we wanted to pay him a friendly visit. He told us that he would be at his country-house, and Caudagna knows where it is."

Her reasons were a mixture of prudence and of love, two feelings which are seldom blended together. My answer was to kiss her with as much admiration as tenderness, and the next day at four o'clock in the afternoon we paid our visit to M. Dubois. We were much surprised, for we found him alone with a very pretty girl, whom he presented to us as his niece.

"I am delighted to see you," he said, "but as I did not expect to see you I altered my arrangements, and instead of the dinner I had intended to give I have invited my friends to supper. I hope you will not refuse me the honour of your company. The two virtuosi will soon be here."

We were compelled to accept his invitation.

"Will there be many guests?" I enquired.

"You will find yourselves in the midst of people worthy of you," he answered, triumphantly. "I am only sorry that I have not invited any ladies."

This polite remark, which was intended for Henriette, made her drop him a curtsy, which she accompanied with a smile. I was pleased to read contentment on her countenance, but, alas! she was concealing the painful anxiety which she felt acutely. Her noble mind refused to shew any uneasiness, and I could not guess her inmost thoughts because I had no idea that she had anything to fear.

I should have thought and acted differently if I had known all her history. Instead of remaining in Parma I should have gone with her to London, and I know now that she would have been delighted to go there.

The two artists arrived soon afterwards; they were the 'primo cantatore' Laschi, and the 'prima donna' Baglioni, then a very pretty woman. The other guests soon followed; all of them were Frenchmen and Spaniards of a certain age. No introductions took place, and I read the tact of the witty hunchback in the omission, but as all the guests were men used to the manners of the court, that neglect of etiquette did not prevent them from paying every honour to my lovely friend, who received their compliments with that ease and good breeding which are known only in France, and even there only in the highest society, with the exception, however, of a few French provinces in which the nobility, wrongly called good society, shew rather too openly the haughtiness which is characteristic of that class.

The concert began by a magnificent symphony, after which Laschi and Baglioni sang a duet with great talent and much taste. They were followed by a pupil of the celebrated Vandini, who played a concerto on the violoncello, and was warmly applauded.

The applause had not yet ceased when Henriette, leaving her seat, went up to the young artist, and told him, with modest confidence, as she took the violoncello from him, that she could bring out the beautiful tone of the instrument still better. I was struck with amazement. She took the young man's seat, placed the violoncello between her knees, and begged the leader of the orchestra to begin the concerto again. The deepest silence prevailed. I was trembling all over, and almost fainting. Fortunately every look was fixed upon Henriette, and nobody thought of me. Nor was she looking towards me, she would not have then ventured even one glance, for she would have lost courage, if she had raised her beautiful eyes to my face. However, not seeing her disposing herself to play, I was beginning to imagine that she had only been indulging in a jest, when she suddenly made the strings resound. My heart was beating with such force that I thought I should drop down dead.

But let the reader imagine my situation when, the concerto being over, well-merited applause burst from every part of the room! The rapid change from extreme fear to excessive pleasure brought on an excitement which was like a violent fever. The applause did not seem to have any effect upon Henriette, who, without raising her eyes from the notes which she saw for the first time, played six pieces with the greatest perfection. As she rose from her seat, she did not thank the guests for their applause, but, addressing the young artist with affability, she told him, with a sweet smile, that she had never played on a finer instrument. Then, curtsying to the audience, she said,

"I entreat your forgiveness for a movement of vanity which has made me encroach on your patience for half an hour."

The nobility and grace of this remark completely upset me, and I ran out to weep like a child, in the garden where no one could see me.

"Who is she, this Henriette?" I said to myself, my heart beating, and my eyes swimming with tears of emotion, "what is this treasure I have in my possession?"

My happiness was so immense that I felt myself unworthy of it.

Lost in these thoughts which enhanced the pleasure of any tears, I should have stayed for a long time in the garden if Dubois had not come out to look for me. He felt anxious about me, owing to my sudden disappearance, and I quieted him by saying that a slight giddiness had compelled me to come out to breathe the fresh air.

Before re-entering the room, I had time to dry my tears, but my eyelids were still red. Henriette, however, was the only one to take notice of it, and she said to me,

"I know, my darling, why you went into the garden!"

She knew me so well that she could easily guess the impression made on my heart by the evening's occurrence.

Dubois had invited the most amiable noblemen of the court, and his supper was dainty and well arranged. I was seated opposite Henriette who was, as a matter of course, monopolizing the general attention, but she would have met with the same success if she had been surrounded by a circle of ladies whom she would certainly have thrown into the shade by her beauty, her wit, and the distinction of her manners. She was the charm of that supper by the animation she imparted to the conversation. M. Dubois said nothing, but he was proud to have such a lovely guest in his house. She contrived to say a few gracious words to everyone, and was shrewd enough never to utter something witty without making me take a share in it. On my side, I openly shewed my submissiveness, my deference, and my respect for that divinity, but it was all in vain. She wanted everybody to know that I was her lord and master. She might have been taken for my wife, but my behaviour to her rendered such a supposition improbable.

The conversation having fallen on the respective merits of the French and Spanish nations, Dubois was foolish enough to ask Henriette to which she gave preference.

It would have been difficult to ask a more indiscreet question, considering that the company was composed almost entirely of Frenchmen and Spaniards in about equal proportion. Yet my Henriette turned the difficulty so cleverly that the Frenchmen would have liked to be Spaniards, and 'vice versa'. Dubois, nothing daunted, begged her to say what she thought of the Italians. The question made me tremble. A certain M. de la Combe, who was seated near me, shook his head in token of disapprobation, but Henriette did not try to elude the question.

"What can I say about the Italians," she answered, "I know only one? If I am to judge them all from that one my judgment must certainly be most favourable to them, but one single example is not sufficient to establish the rule."

It was impossible to give a better answer, but as my readers may well imagine, I did not appear to have heard it, and being anxious to prevent any more indiscreet questions from Dubois I turned the conversation into a different channel.

The subject of music was discussed, and a Spaniard asked Henriette whether she could play any other instrument besides the violoncello.

"No," she answered, "I never felt any inclination for any other. I learned the violoncello at the convent to please my mother, who can play it pretty well, and without an order from my father, sanctioned by the bishop, the abbess would never have given me permission to practise it."

"What objection could the abbess make?"

"That devout spouse of our Lord pretended that I could not play that instrument without assuming an indecent position."

At this the Spanish guests bit their lips, but the Frenchmen laughed heartily, and did not spare their epigrams against the over-particular abbess.

After a short silence, Henriette rose, and we all followed her example. It was the signal for breaking up the party, and we soon took our leave.

I longed to find myself alone with the idol of my soul. I asked her a hundred questions without waiting for the answers.

"Ah! you were right, my own Henriette, when you refused to go to that concert, for you knew that you would raise many enemies against me. I am certain that all those men hate me, but what do I care? You are my universe! Cruel darling, you almost killed me with your violoncello, because, having no idea of your being a musician, I thought you had gone mad, and when I heard you I was compelled to leave the room in order to weep undisturbed. My tears relieved my fearful oppression. Oh! I entreat you to tell me what other talents you possess. Tell me candidly, for you might kill me if you brought them out unexpectedly, as you have done this evening."

"I have no other accomplishments, my best beloved. I have emptied my bag all at once. Now you know your Henriette entirely. Had you not chanced to tell me about a month ago that you had no taste for music, I would have told you that I could play the violoncello remarkably well, but if I had mentioned such a thing, I know you well enough to be certain that you would have bought an instrument immediately, and I could not, dearest, find pleasure in anything that would weary you."

The very next morning she had an excellent violoncello, and, far from wearying me, each time she played she caused me a new and greater pleasure. I believe that it would be impossible even to a man disliking music not to become passionately fond of it, if that art were practised to perfection by the woman he adores.

The 'vox humana' of the violoncello, the king of instruments, went to my heart every time that my beloved Henriette performed upon it. She knew I loved to hear her play, and every day she afforded me that pleasure. Her talent delighted me so much that I proposed to her to give some concerts, but she was prudent enough to refuse my proposal. But in spite of all her prudence we had no power to hinder the decrees of fate.

The fatal hunchback came the day after his fine supper to thank us and to receive our well-merited praises of his concert, his supper, and the distinction of his guests.

"I foresee, madam," he said to Henriette, "all the difficulty I shall have in defending myself against the prayers of all my friends, who will beg of me to introduce them to you."

"You need not have much trouble on that score: you know that I never, receive anyone."

Dubois did not again venture upon speaking of introducing any friend.

On the same day I received a letter from young Capitani, in which he informed me that, being the owner of St. Peter's knife and sheath, he had called on Franzia with two learned magicians who had promised to raise the treasure out of the earth, and that to his great surprise Franzia had refused to receive him: He entreated me to write to the worthy fellow, and to go to him myself if I wanted to have my share of the treasure. I need not say that I did not comply with his wishes, but I can vouch for the real pleasure I felt in finding that I had succeeded in saving that honest and simple farmer from the impostors who would have ruined him.

One month was gone since the great supper given by Dubois. We had passed it in all the enjoyment which can be derived both from the senses and the mind, and never had one single instant of weariness caused either of us to be guilty of that sad symptom of misery which is called a yawn. The only pleasure we took out of doors was a drive outside of the city when the weather was fine. As we never walked in the streets, and never frequented any public place, no one had sought to make our acquaintance, or at least no one had found an opportunity of doing so, in spite of all the curiosity excited by Henriette amongst the persons whom we had chanced to meet, particularly at the house of Dubois. Henriette had become more courageous, and I more confident, when we found that she had not been recognized by any one either at that supper or at the theatre. She only dreaded persons belonging to the high nobility.

One day as we were driving outside the Gate of Colorno, we met the duke and duchess who were returning to Parma. Immediately after their carriage another vehicle drove along, in which was Dubois with a nobleman unknown to us. Our carriage had only gone a few yards from theirs when one of our horses broke down. The companion of Dubois immediately ordered his coachman to stop in order to send to our assistance. Whilst the horse was raised again, he came politely to our carriage, and paid some civil compliment to Henriette. M. Dubois, always a shrewd courtier and anxious to shew off at the expense of others, lost no time in introducing him as M. Dutillot, the French ambassador. My sweetheart gave the conventional bow. The horse being all right again, we proceeded on our road after thanking the gentlemen for their courtesy. Such an every-day occurrence could not be expected to have any serious consequences, but alas! the most important events are often the result of very trifling circumstances!

The next day, Dubois breakfasted with us. He told us frankly that M. Dutillot had been delighted at the fortunate chance which had afforded him an opportunity of making our acquaintance, and that he had entreated him to ask our permission to call on us.

"On madam or on me?" I asked at once.

"On both."

"Very well, but one at a time. Madam, as you know, has her own room and I have mine."

"Yes, but they are so near each other!"

"Granted, yet I must tell you that, as far as I am concerned, I should have much pleasure in waiting upon his excellency if he should ever wish to communicate with me, and you will oblige me by letting him know it. As for madam, she is here, speak to her, my dear M. Dubois, for I am only her very humble servant."

Henriette assumed an air of cheerful politeness, and said to him,

"Sir, I beg you will offer my thanks to M. Dutillot, and enquire from him whether he knows me."

"I am certain, madam," said the hunchback, "that he does not."

"You see he does not know me, and yet he wishes to call on me. You must agree with me that if I accepted his visits I should give him a singular opinion of my character. Be good enough to tell him that, although known to no one and knowing no one, I am not an adventuress, and therefore I must decline the honour of his visits."

Dubois felt that he had taken a false step, and remained silent. We never asked him how the ambassador had received our refusal.

Three weeks after the last occurrence, the ducal court residing then at Colorno, a great entertainment was given in the gardens which were to be illuminated all night. Everybody had permission to walk about the gardens. Dubois, the fatal hunchback appointed by destiny, spoke so much of that festival, that we took a fancy to see it. Always the same story of Adam's apple. Dubois accompanied us. We went to Colorno the day before the entertainment, and put up at an inn.

In the evening we walked through the gardens, in which we happened to meet the ducal family and suite. According to the etiquette of the French court, Madame de France was the first to curtsy to Henriette, without stopping. My eyes fell upon a gentleman walking by the side of Don Louis, who was looking at my friend very attentively. A few minutes after, as we were retracing our steps, we came across the same gentleman who, after bowing respectfully to us, took Dubois aside. They conversed together for a quarter of an hour, following us all the time, and we were passing out of the gardens, when the gentleman, coming forward, and politely apologizing to me, asked Henriette whether he had the honour to be known to her.

"I do not recollect having ever had the honour of seeing you before."

"That is enough, madam, and I entreat you to forgive me."

Dubois informed us that the gentleman was the intimate friend of the Infante Don Louis, and that, believing he knew madam, he had begged to be introduced. Dubois had answered that her name was D'Arci, and that, if he was known to the lady, he required no introduction. M. d'Antoine said that the name of D'Arci was unknown to him, and that he was afraid of making a mistake. "In that state of doubt," added Dubois, "and wishing to clear it, he introduced himself, but now he must see that he was mistaken."

After supper, Henriette appeared anxious. I asked her whether she had only pretended not to know M. d'Antoine.

"No, dearest, I can assure you. I know his name which belongs to an illustrious family of Provence, but I have never seen him before."

"Perhaps he may know you?"

"He might have seen me, but I am certain that he never spoke to me, or I would have recollected him."

"That meeting causes me great anxiety, and it seems to have troubled you."

"I confess it has disturbed my mind."

"Let us leave Parma at once and proceed to Genoa. We will go to Venice as soon as my affairs there are settled."

"Yes, my dear friend, we shall then feel more comfortable. But I do not think we need be in any hurry."

We returned to Parma, and two days afterwards my servant handed me a letter, saying that the footman who had brought it was waiting in the ante-room.

"This letter," I said to Henriette, "troubles me."

She took it, and after she had read it—she gave it back to me, saying,

"I think M. d'Antoine is a man of honour, and I hope that we may have nothing to fear."

The letter ran as, follows:

"Either at your hotel or at my residence, or at any other place you may wish to appoint, I entreat you, sir, to give me an opportunity of conversing with you on a subject which must be of the greatest importance to you.

"I have the honour to be, etc.

"D'Antoine."

It was addressed M. Farusi.

"I think I must see him," I said, "but where?"

"Neither here nor at his residence, but in the ducal gardens. Your answer must name only the place and the hour of the meeting."

I wrote to M. d'Antoine that I would see him at half-past eleven in the ducal gardens, only requesting him to appoint another hour in case mine was not convenient to him.

I dressed myself at once in order to be in good time, and meanwhile we both endeavoured, Henriette and I, to keep a cheerful countenance, but we could not silence our sad forebodings. I was exact to my appointment and found M. d'Antoine waiting for me. As soon as we were together, he said to me,

"I have been compelled, sir, to beg from you the favour of an interview, because I could not imagine any surer way to get this letter to

Madame d'Arci's hands. I entreat you to deliver it to her, and to excuse me if I give it you sealed. Should I be mistaken, my letter will not even require an answer, but should I be right, Madame d'Arci alone can judge whether she ought to communicate it to you. That is my reason for giving it to you sealed. If you are truly her friend, the contents of that letter must be as interesting to you as to her. May I hope, sir, that you will be good enough to deliver it to her?"

"Sir, on my honour I will do it."

We bowed respectfully to each other, and parted company. I hurried back to the hotel.

III

Henriette Receives the Visit of M. D'Antoine I Accompany Her as Far as Geneva and Then I Lose Her—I Cross the St. Bernard, and Return to Parma—A Letter from Hensiette—My Despair De La Haye Becomes Attached to Me—Unpleasant Adventure with an Actress and Its Consequences—I Turn a Thorough Bigot—Bavois—I Mystify a Bragging Officer.

As soon as I had reached our apartment, my heart bursting with anxiety, I repeated to Henriette every word spoken by M. d'Antoine, and delivered his letter which contained four pages of writing. She read it attentively with visible emotion, and then she said,

"Dearest friend, do not be offended, but the honour of two families does not allow of my imparting to you the contents of this letter. I am compelled to receive M. d'Antoine, who represents himself as being one of my relatives."

"Ah!" I exclaimed, "this is the beginning of the end! What a dreadful thought! I am near the end of a felicity which was too great to last! Wretch that I have been! Why did I tarry so long in Parma? What fatal blindness! Of all the cities in the whole world, except France, Parma was the only one I had to fear, and it is here that I have brought you, when I could have taken you anywhere else, for you had no will but mine! I am all the more guilty that you never concealed your fears from me. Why did I introduce that fatal Dubois here? Ought I not to have guessed that his curiosity would sooner or later prove injurious to us? And yet I cannot condemn that curiosity, for it is, alas! a natural feeling. I can only accuse all the perfections which Heaven has bestowed upon you!—perfections which have caused my happiness, and which will plunge me in an abyss of despair, for, alas! I foresee a future of fearful misery."

"I entreat you, dearest, to foresee nothing, and to calm yourself. Let us avail ourselves of all our reason in order to prove ourselves superior to circumstances, whatever they may be. I cannot answer this letter, but you must write to M. d'Antoine to call here tomorrow and to send up his name."

"Alas! you compel me to perform a painful task."

"You are my best, my only friend; I demand nothing, I impose no task upon you, but can you refuse me?"

"No, never, no matter what you ask. Dispose of me, I am yours in life and death."

"I knew what you would answer. You must be with me when M. d'Antoine calls, but after a few minutes given to etiquette, will you find some pretext to go to your room, and leave us alone? M. d'Antoine knows all my history; he knows in what I have done wrong, in what I have been right; as a man of honour, as my relative, he must shelter me from all affront. He shall not do anything against my will, and if he attempts to deviate from the conditions I will dictate to him, I will refuse to go to France, I will follow you anywhere, and devote to you the remainder of my life. Yet, my darling, recollect that some fatal circumstances may compel us to consider our separation as the wisest course to adopt, that we must husband all our courage to adopt it, if necessary, and to endeavour not to be too unhappy.

"Have confidence in me, and be quite certain that I shall take care to reserve for myself the small portion of happiness which I can be allowed to enjoy without the man who alone has won all my devoted love. You will have, I trust, and I expect it from your generous soul, the same care of your future, and I feel certain that you must succeed. In the mean time, let us drive away all the sad forebodings which might darken the hours we have yet before us."

"Ah! why did we not go away immediately after we had met that accursed favourite of the Infante!"

"We might have made matters much worse; for in that case M. d'Antoine might have made up his mind to give my family a proof of his zeal by instituting a search to discover our place of residence, and I should then have been exposed to violent proceedings which you would not have endured. It would have been fatal to both of us."

I did everything she asked me. From that moment our love became sad, and sadness is a disease which gives the death-blow to affection. We would often remain a whole hour opposite each other without exchanging a single word, and our sighs would be heard whatever we did to hush them.

The next day, when M. d'Antoine called, I followed exactly the instructions she had given me, and for six mortal hours I remained alone, pretending to write.

The door of my room was open, and a large looking-glass allowed us to see each other. They spent those six hours in writing, occasionally stopping to talk of I do not know what, but their conversation was evidently a decisive one. The reader can easily realize how much I suffered during that long torture, for I could expect nothing but the total wreck of my happiness.

As soon as the terrible M. d'Antoine had taken leave of her, Henriette came to me, and observing that her eyes were red I heaved a deep sigh, but she tried to smile.

"Shall we go away to-morrow, dearest?"

"Oh! yes, I am ready. Where do you wish me to take you?"

"Anywhere you like, but we must be here in a fortnight."

"Here! Oh, fatal illusion!"

"Alas! it is so. I have promised to be here to receive the answer to a letter I have just written. We have no violent proceedings to fear, but I cannot bear to remain in Parma."

"Ah! I curse the hour which brought us to this city. Would you like to go to Milan?"

"Yes."

"As we are unfortunately compelled to come back, we may as well take with us Caudagna and his sister."

"As you please."

"Let me arrange everything. I will order a carriage for them, and they will take charge of your violoncello. Do you not think that you ought to let M. d'Antoine know where we are going?"

"No, it seems to me, on the contrary, that I need not account to him for any of my proceedings. So much the worse for him if he should, even for one moment, doubt my word."

The next morning, we left Parma, taking only what we wanted for an absence of a fortnight. We arrived in Milan without accident, but both very sad, and we spent the following fifteen days in constant tete-a-tete, without speaking to anyone, except the landlord of the hotel and to a dressmaker. I presented my beloved Henriette with a magnificent pelisse made of lynx fur—a present which she prized highly.

Out of delicacy, she had never enquired about my means, and I felt grateful to her for that reserve. I was very careful to conceal from her the fact that my purse was getting very light. When we came back to Parma I had only three or four hundred sequins.

The day after our return M. d'Antoine invited himself to dine with us, and after we had drunk coffee, I left him alone with Henriette. Their interview was as long as the first, and our separation was decided. She informed me of it, immediately after the departure of M. d'Antoine, and for a long time we remained folded in each other's arms, silent, and blending our bitter tears.

"When shall I have to part from you, my beloved, alas! too much beloved one?"

"Be calm, dearest, only when we reach Geneva, whither you are going to accompany me. Will you try to find me a respectable maid by to-morrow? She will accompany me from Geneva to the place where I am bound to go."

"Oh! then, we shall spend a few days more together! I know no one but Dubois whom I could trust to procure a good femme-de-chambre; only I do not want him to learn from her what you might not wish him to know."

"That will not be the case, for I will take another maid as soon as I am in France."

Three days afterwards, Dubois, who had gladly undertaken the commission, presented to Henriette a woman already somewhat advanced in years, pretty well dressed and respectable-looking, who, being poor, was glad of an opportunity of going back to France, her native country. Her husband, an old military officer, had died a few months before, leaving her totally unprovided for. Henriette engaged her, and told her to keep herself ready to start whenever M. Dubois should give her notice. The day before the one fixed for our departure, M. d'Antoine dined with us, and, before taking leave of us, he gave Henriette a sealed letter for Geneva.

We left Parma late in the evening, and stopped only two hours in Turin, in order to engage a manservant whose services we required as far as Geneva. The next day we ascended Mont Cenis in sedan-chairs, and we descended to the Novalaise in mountain-sledges. On the fifth day we reached Geneva, and we put up at the Hotel des Balances. The next morning, Henriette gave me a letter for the banker Tronchin, who, when he had read it, told me that he would call himself at the hotel, and bring me one thousand louis d'or.

I came back and we sat down to dinner. We had not finished our meal when the banker was announced. He had brought the thousand louis d'or, and told Henriette that he would give her two men whom he could recommend in every way.

She answered that she would leave Geneva as soon as she had the carriage which he was to provide for her, according to the letter

I had delivered to him. He promised that everything would be ready for the following day, and he left us. It was indeed a terrible moment! Grief almost benumbed us both. We remained motionless, speechless, wrapped up in the most profound despair.

I broke that sad silence to tell her that the carriage which M. Tronchin would provide could not possibly be as comfortable and as safe as mine, and I entreated her to take it, assuring her that by accepting it she would give me a last proof of her affection.

"I will take in exchange, my dearest love, the carriage sent by the banker."

"I accept the change, darling," she answered, "it will be a great consolation to possess something which has belonged to you."

As she said these words, she slipped in my pocket five rolls containing each one hundred louis d'or—a slight consolation for my heart, which was almost broken by our cruel separation! During the last twenty-four hours we could boast of no other eloquence but that which finds expression in tears, in sobs, and in those hackneyed but energetic exclamations, which two happy lovers are sure to address to reason, when in its sternness it compels them to part from one another in the very height of their felicity. Henriette did not endeavour to lure me with any hope for the future, in order to allay my sorrow! Far from that, she said to me,

"Once we are parted by fate, my best and only friend, never enquire after me, and, should chance throw you in my way, do not appear to know me."

She gave me a letter for M. d'Antoine, without asking me whether I intended to go back to Parma, but, even if such had not been my intention, I should have determined at once upon returning to that city. She likewise entreated me not to leave Geneva until I had received a letter which she promised to, write to me from the first stage on her journey. She started at day-break, having with her a maid, a footman on the box of the carriage, and being preceded by a courier on horseback. I followed her with my eyes as long as I could, see her carriage, and I was still standing on the same spot long after my eyes had lost sight of it. All my thoughts were wrapped up in the beloved object I had lost for ever. The world was a blank!

I went back to my room, ordered the waiter not to disturb me until the return of the horses which had drawn Henriette's carriage, and I lay down on my bed in the hope that sleep would for a time silence a grief which tears could not drown.

The postillion who had driven Henriette did not return till the next day; he had gone as far as Chatillon. He brought me a letter in which I found one single word: Adieu! He told me that they had reached Chatillon without accident, and that the lady had immediately continued her journey towards Lyons. As I could not leave Geneva until the following day, I spent alone in my room some of the most melancholy hours of my life. I saw on one of the panes of glass of a window these words which she had traced with the point of a diamond I had given her: "You will forget Henriette." That prophecy was not likely to afford me any consolation. But had she attached its full meaning to the word "forget?" No; she could only mean that time would at last heal the deep wounds of my heart, and she ought not to have made it deeper by leaving behind her those words which sounded like a reproach. No, I have not forgotten her, for even now, when my head is covered with white hair, the recollection of her is still a source of happiness for my heart! When I think that in my old age I derive happiness only from my recollections of the past, I find that my long life must have counted more bright than dark days, and offering my thanks to God, the Giver of all, I congratulate myself, and confess that life is a great blessing.

The next day I set off again for Italy with a servant recommended by M. Tronchin, and although the season was not favourable I took the road over Mont St. Bernard, which I crossed in three days, with seven mules carrying me, my servant, my luggage, and the carriage sent by the banker to the beloved woman now for ever lost to me. One of the advantages of a great sorrow is that nothing else seems painful. It is a sort of despair which is not without some sweetness. During that journey I never felt either hunger or thirst, or the cold which is so intense in that part of the Alps that the whole of nature seems to turn to ice, or the fatigue inseparable from such a difficult and dangerous journey.

I arrived in Parma in pretty good health, and took up my quarters at a small inn, in the hope that in such a place I should not meet any acquaintance of mine. But I was much disappointed, for I found in that inn M. de la Haye, who had a room next to mine. Surprised at seeing me, he paid me a long compliment, trying to make me speak, but I eluded his curiosity by telling him that I was tired, and that we would see each other again.

On the following day I called upon M. d'Antoine, and delivered the letter which Henriette had written to him. He opened it in my presence, and finding another to my address enclosed in his, he handed it to me without reading it, although it was not sealed. Thinking, however, that it might have been Henriette's intention that he should read it because it was open, he asked my permission to do so, which I granted with pleasure as soon as I had myself perused it. He handed it back to me after he had read it, telling me very feelingly that I could in everything rely upon him and upon his influence and credit.

Here is Henriette's letter

"It is I, dearest and best friend, who have been compelled to abandon you, but do not let your grief be increased by any thought of my sorrow. Let us be wise enough to suppose that we have had a happy dream, and not to complain of destiny, for never did so beautiful a dream last so long! Let us be proud of the consciousness that for three months we gave one another the most perfect felicity. Few human beings can boast of so much! Let us swear never to forget one another, and to often remember the happy hours of our love, in order to renew them in our souls, which, although divided, will enjoy them as acutely as if our hearts were beating one against the other. Do not make any enquiries about me, and if chance should let you know who I am, forget it for ever. I feel certain that you will be glad to hear that I have arranged my affairs so well that I shall, for the remainder of my life, be as happy as I can possibly be without you, dear friend, by my side. I do not know who you are, but I am certain that no one in the world knows you better than I do. I shall not have another lover as long as I live, but I do not wish you to imitate me. On the contrary I hope that you will love again, and I trust that a good fairy will bring along your path another Henriette. Farewell... farewell."

I MET THAT ADORABLE WOMAN fifteen years later; the reader will see where and how, when we come to that period of my life.

I WENT BACK TO MY room, careless of the future, broken down by the deepest of sorrows, I locked myself in, and went to bed. I felt so low in spirits that I was stunned. Life was not a burden, but only because I did not give a thought to life. In fact I was in a state of complete apathy, moral and physical. Six years later I found myself in a similar predicament, but that time love was not the cause of my sorrow; it was the horrible and too famous prison of The Leads, in Venice.

I was not much better either in 1768, when I was lodged in the prison of Buen Retiro, in Madrid, but I must not anticipate events. At the end of twenty-four hours, my exhaustion was very great, but I did not find the sensation disagreeable, and, in the state of mind in which I was then, I was pleased with the idea that, by increasing, that weakness would at last kill me. I was delighted to see that no one disturbed me to offer me some food, and I congratulated myself upon having dismissed my servant. Twenty-four more hours passed by, and my weakness became complete inanition.

I was in that state when De la Haye knocked at my door. I would not have answered if he had not said that someone insisted upon seeing me. I got out of bed, and, scarcely able to stand, I opened my door, after which I got into bed again.

"There is a stranger here," he said, "who, being in want of a carriage, offers to buy yours."

"I do not want to sell it."

"Excuse me if I have disturbed you, but you look ill."

"Yes, I wish to be left alone."

"What is the matter with you?"

Coming nearer my bed, he took my hand, and found my pulse extremely low and weak.

"What did you eat yesterday?"

"I have eaten nothing, thank God I for two days."

Guessing the real state of things, De la Haye became anxious, and entreated me to take some broth. He threw so much kindness, so much unction, into his entreaties that, through weakness and weariness, I allowed myself to be persuaded. Then, without ever mentioning the name of Henriette, he treated me to a sermon upon the life to come, upon the vanity of the things of this life which we are foolish enough to prefer, and upon the necessity of respecting our existence, which does not belong to us.

I was listening without answering one word, but, after all, I was listening, and De la Haye, perceiving his advantage, would not leave me, and ordered dinner. I had neither the will nor the strength to resist, and when the dinner was served, I ate something. Then De la Have saw that he had conquered, and for the remainder of the day devoted himself to amusing me by his cheerful conversation.

The next day the tables were turned, for it was I who invited him to keep me company and to dine with me. It seemed to me that I had not lost a particle of my sadness, but life appeared to me once more preferable to death, and, thinking that I was indebted to him for the preservation of my life, I made a great friend of him. My readers will see presently that my affection for him went very far, and they will, like me, marvel at the cause of that friendship, and at the means through which it was brought about.

Three or four days afterwards, Dubois, who had been informed of everything by De la Haye, called on me, and persuaded me to go out. I went to the theatre, where I made the acquaintance of several Corsican officers, who had served in France, in the Royal Italian regiment. I also met a young man from Sicily, named Paterno, the wildest and most heedless fellow it was possible to see. He was in love with an actress who made a fool of him. He amused me with the enumeration of all her adorable qualities, and of all the cruelties she was practising upon him, for, although she received him at all hours, she repulsed him harshly whenever he tried to steal the slightest favour. In the mean time, she ruined him by making him pay constantly for excellent dinners and suppers, which were eaten by her family, but which did not advance him one inch towards the fulfilment of his wishes.

He succeeded at last in exciting my curiosity. I examined the actress on the stage, and finding that she was not without beauty I expressed a wish to know her. Paterno was delighted to introduce me to her.

I found that she was of tolerably easy virtue, and, knowing that she was very far from rolling in riches, I had no doubt that fifteen or twenty sequins would be quite sufficient to make her compliant. I communicated my thoughts to Paterno, but he laughed and told me that, if I dared to make such a proposition to her, she would certainly shut her door against me. He named several officers whom she had refused to receive again, because they had made similar offers.

"Yet," added the young man, "I wish you would make the attempt, and tell me the result candidly."

I felt piqued, and promised to do it.

I paid her a visit in her dressing-room at the theatre, and as she happened during our conversation to praise the beauty of my watch, I told her that she could easily obtain possession of it, and I said at what price. She answered, according to the catechism of her profession, that an honourable man had no right to make such an offer to a respectable girl.

"I offer only one ducat," said I, "to those who are not respectable."

And I left her.

When I told Paterno what had occurred, he fairly jumped for joy, but I knew what to think of it all, for 'cosi sono tutte', and in spite of all his entreaties, I declined to be present at his suppers, which were far from amusing, and gave the family of the actress an opportunity of laughing at the poor fool who was paying for them.

Seven or eight days afterwards, Paterno told me that the actress had related the affair to him exactly in the same words which I had used, and she had added that, if I had ceased my visits, it was only because I was afraid of her taking me at my word in case I should renew my proposal. I commissioned him to tell her that I would pay her another visit, not to renew my offer, but to shew my contempt for any proposal she might make me herself.

The heedless fellow fulfilled his commission so well that the actress, feeling insulted, told him that she dared me to call on her. Perfectly determined to shew that I despised her, I went to her dressing-room the same evening, after the second act of a play in which she had not to appear again. She dismissed those who were with her, saying that she wanted to speak with me, and, after she had bolted the door, she sat down gracefully on my knees, asking me whether it was true that I despised her so much.

In such a position a man has not the courage to insult a woman, and, instead of answering, I set to work at once, without meeting even with that show of resistance which sharpens the appetite. In spite of that, dupe as I always was of a feeling truly absurd when an intelligent man has to deal with such creatures, I gave her twenty sequins, and I confess that it was paying dearly for very smarting regrets. We both laughed at the stupidity of Paterno, who did not seem to know how such challenges generally end.

I saw the unlucky son of Sicily the next morning, and I told him that, having found the actress very dull, I would not see her again. Such was truly my intention, but a very important reason, which nature took care to explain to me three days afterwards, compelled me to keep my word through a much more serious motive than a simple dislike for the woman.

However, although I was deeply grieved to find myself in such a disgraceful position, I did not think I had any right to complain. On the contrary, I considered that my misfortune to be a just and well-deserved punishment for having abandoned myself to a Lais, after I had enjoyed the felicity of possessing a woman like Henriette.

My disease was not a case within the province of empirics, and I bethought myself of confiding in M. de is Haye who was then dining every day with me, and made no mystery of his poverty. He placed me in the hands of a skilful surgeon, who was at the same time a dentist. He recognized certain symptoms which made it a necessity to sacrifice me to the god Mercury, and that treatment, owing to the season of the year, compelled me to keep my room for six weeks. It was during the winter of 1749.

While I was thus curing myself of an ugly disease, De la Haye inoculated me with another as bad, perhaps even worse, which I should never have thought myself susceptible of catching. This Fleming, who left me only for one hour in the morning, to go—at least he said so—to church to perform his devotions, made a bigot of me! And to such an extent, that I agreed with him that I was indeed fortunate to have caught a disease which was the origin of the faith now taking possession of my soul. I would thank God fervently and with the most complete conviction for having employed Mercury to lead my mind, until then wrapped in darkness, to the pure light of holy truth! There is no doubt that such an extraordinary change in my reasoning system was the result of the exhaustion brought on by the mercury. That impure and always injurious metal had weakened my mind to such an extent that I had become almost besotted, and I fancied that until then my judgment had been insane. The result was that, in my newly acquired wisdom, I took the resolution of leading a totally different sort of life in future. De la Haye would often cry for joy when he saw me shedding tears caused by the contrition which he had had the wonderful cleverness to sow in my poor sickly soul. He would talk to me of paradise and the other world, just as if he had visited them in person, and I never laughed at him! He had accustomed me to renounce my reason; now to renounce that divine faculty a man must no longer be conscious of its value, he must have become an idiot. The reader may judge of the state to which I was reduced by the following specimen. One day, De la Haye said to me:

"It is not known whether God created the world during the vernal equinox or during the autumnal one."

"Creation being granted," I replied, in spite of the mercury, "such a question is childish, for the seasons are relative, and differ in the different quarters of the globe."

De la Haye reproached me with the heathenism of my ideas, told me that I must abandon such impious reasonings... and I gave way!

That man had been a Jesuit. He not only, however, refused to admit it, but he would not even suffer anyone to mention it to him. This is how he completed his work of seduction by telling me the history of his life.

"After I had been educated in a good school," he said, "and had devoted myself with some success to the arts and sciences, I was for twenty years employed at the University of Paris. Afterwards I served as an engineer in the army, and since that time I have published several works anonymously, which are now in use in every boys' school. Having given up the military service, and being poor, I undertook and completed the education of several young men, some of whom shine now in the world even more by their excellent conduct than by their talents. My last pupil was the Marquis Botta. Now being without employment I live, as you see, trusting in God's providence. Four years ago, I made the acquaintance of Baron Bavois, from Lausanne, son of General Bavois who commanded a regiment in the service of the Duke of Modem, and afterwards was unfortunate enough to make himself too conspicuous. The young baron, a Calvinist like his father, did not like the idle life he was leading at home, and he solicited me to undertake his education in order to fit him for a military career. Delighted at the opportunity of cultivating his fine natural disposition, I gave up everything to devote myself entirely to my task. I soon discovered that, in the question of faith, he knew himself to be in error, and that he remained a Calvinist only out of respect to his family. When I had found out his secret feelings on that head, I had no difficulty in proving to him that his most important interests were involved in that question, as his eternal salvation was at stake. Struck by the truth of my words, he abandoned himself to my affection, and I took him to Rome, where I presented him to the Pope, Benedict XIV, who, immediately after the abjuration of my pupil got him a lieutenancy in the army of the Duke of Modena. But the dear proselyte, who is only twenty-five years of age, cannot live upon his pay of seven sequins a month, and since his abjuration he has received nothing from his parents, who are highly incensed at what they call his apostasy. He would find himself compelled to go back to Lausanne, if I did not assist him. But, alas! I am poor, and without employment, so I can only send him the trifling sums which I can obtain from the few good Christians with whom I am acquainted.

"My pupil, whose heart is full of gratitude, would be very glad to know his benefactors, but they refuse to acquaint him with their names, and they are right, because charity, in order to be meritorious, must not partake of any feeling of vanity. Thank God, I have no cause for such a feeling! I am but too happy to act as a father towards a young saint, and to have had a share, as the humble instrument of the Almighty, in the salvation of his soul. That handsome and good young man trusts no one but me, and writes to me regularly twice a week. I am too discreet to communicate his letters to you, but, if you were to read them, they would make you weep for sympathy. It is to him that I have sent the three gold pieces which you gave me yesterday."

As he said the last words my converter rose, and went to the window to dry his tears, I felt deeply moved, anal full of admiration for the virtue of De la Haye and of his pupil, who, to save his soul, had placed himself under the hard necessity of accepting alms. I cried as well as the apostle, and in my dawning piety I told him that I insisted not only upon remaining unknown to his pupil, but also upon ignoring the amount of the sums he might take out of my purse to forward to him, and I therefore begged that he would help himself without rendering me any account. De la Haye embraced me warmly, saying that, by following the precepts of the Gospel so well, I should certainly win the kingdom of heaven.

The mind is sure to follow the body; it is a privilege enjoyed by matter. With an empty stomach, I became a fanatic; and the hollow made in my brain by the mercury became the home of enthusiasm. Without mentioning it to De la Haye, I wrote to my three friends, Messrs. Bragadin and company, several letters full of pathos concerning my Tartufe and his pupil, and I managed to communicate my fanaticism to them. You are aware, dear reader, that nothing is so catching as the plague; now, fanaticism, no matter of what nature, is only the plague of the human mind.

I made my friends to understand that the good of our society depended upon the admission of these two virtuous individuals. I allowed them to guess it, but, having myself became a Jesuit, I took care not to say it openly. It would of course be better if such an idea appeared to have emanated from those men, so simple, and at the same time so truly virtuous. "It is God's will," I wrote to them (for deceit must always take refuge under the protection of that sacred name), "that you employ all your influence in Venice to find an honourable position for M. de la Haye, and to promote the interests of young M. Bavois in his profession."

M. de Bragadin answered that De la Haye could take up his quarters with us in his palace, and that Bavois was to write to his protector, the Pope, entreating His Holiness to recommend him to the ambassador of Venice, who would then forward that recommendation to the Senate, and that Bavois could, in that way, feel sure of good employment.

The affair of the Patriarchate of Aquileia was at that time under discussion; the Republic of Venice was in possession of it as well as the Emperor of Austria, who claimed the 'jus eligendi': the Pope Benedict XIV had been chosen as arbitrator, and as he had not yet given his decision it was evident that the Republic would shew very great deference to his recommendation.

While that important affair was enlisting all our sympathies, and while they were expecting in Venice a letter stating the effect of the Pope's recommendation, I was the hero of a comic adventure which, for the sake of my readers, must not pass unnoticed.

At the beginning of April I was entirely cured of my last misfortune. I had recovered all my usual vigour, and I accompanied my converter to church every day, never missing a sermon. We likewise spent the evening together at the cafe, where we generally met a great many officers. There was among them a Provencal who amused everybody with his boasting and with the recital of the military exploits by which he pretended to have distinguished himself in the service of several countries, and principally in Spain. As he was truly a source of amusement, everybody pretended to believe him in order to keep up the game. One day as I was staring at him, he asked me whether I knew him.

"By George, sir!"—I exclaimed, "know you! Why, did we not fight side by side at the battle of Arbela?"

At those words everybody burst out laughing, but the boaster, nothing daunted, said, with animation,

"Well, gentlemen, I do not see anything so very laughable in that. I was at that battle, and therefore this gentleman might very well have remarked me; in fact, I think I can recollect him."

And, continuing to speak to me, he named the regiment in which we were brother officers. Of course we embraced one another, congratulating each other upon the pleasure we both felt in meeting again in Parma. After that truly comic joke I left the coffee-room in the company of my inseparable preacher.

The next morning, as I was at breakfast with De la Haye, the boasting Provencal entered my room without taking off his hat, and said,

"M. d'Arbela, I have something of importance to tell you; make haste and follow me. If you are afraid, you may take anyone you please with you. I am good for half a dozen men."

I left my chair, seized my pistols, and aimed at him.

"No one," I said, with decision, "has the right to come and disturb me in my room; be off this minute, or I blow your brains out."

The fellow, drawing his sword, dared me to murder him, but at the same moment De la Haye threw himself between us, stamping violently on the floor. The landlord came up, and threatened the officer to send for the police if he did not withdraw immediately.

He went away, saying that I had insulted him in public, and that he would take care that the reparation I owed him should be as public as the insult.

When he had gone, seeing that the affair might take a tragic turn, I began to examine with De la Haye how it could be avoided, but we had not long to puzzle our imagination, for in less than half an hour an officer of the Infante of Parma presented himself, and requested me to repair immediately to head-quarters, where M. de Bertolan, Commander of Parma, wanted to speak to me.

I asked De la Haye to accompany me as a witness of what I had said in the coffee-room as well as of what had taken place in my apartment.

I presented myself before the commander, whom I found surrounded by several officers, and, among them, the bragging Provencal.

M. de Bertolan, who was a witty man, smiled when he saw me; then, with a very serious countenance, he said to me,

"Sir, as you have made a laughing-stock of this officer in a public place, it is but right that you should give him publicly the satisfaction which he claims, and as commander of this city I find myself bound in duty to ask you for that satisfaction in order to settle the affair amicably."

"Commander," I answered, "I do not see why a satisfaction should be offered to this gentleman, for it is not true that I have insulted him by turning him into ridicule. I told him that I had seen him at the battle of Arbela, and I could not have any doubt about it when he said that he had been present at that battle, and that he knew me again."

"Yes," interrupted the officer, "but I heard Rodela and not Arbela, and everybody knows that I fought at Rodela. But you said Arbela, and certainly with the intention of laughing at me, since that battle has been fought more than two thousand years ago, while the battle of Rodela in Africa took place in our time, and I was there under the orders of the Duke de Mortemar."

"In the first place, sir, you have no right to judge of my intentions, but I do not dispute your having been present at Rodela, since you say so; but in that case the tables are turned, and now I demand a reparation from you if you dare discredit my having been at Arbela. I certainly did not serve under the Duke de Mortemar, because he was not there, at least to my knowledge, but I was aid-de-camp of Parmenion, and I was wounded under his eyes. If you were to ask me to shew you the scar, I could not satisfy you, for you must understand that the body I had at that time does not exist any longer, and in my present bodily envelope I am only twenty-three years old."

"All this seems to me sheer madness, but, at all events, I have witnesses to prove that you have been laughing at me, for you stated that you had seen me at that battle, and, by the powers! it is not possible, because I was not there. At all events, I demand satisfaction."

"So do I, and we have equal rights, if mine are not even better than yours, for your witnesses are likewise mine, and these gentlemen will assert that you said that you had seen me at Rodela, and, by the powers! it is not possible, for I was not there."

"Well, I may have made a mistake."

"So may I, and therefore we have no longer any claim against one another."

The commander, who was biting his lips to restrain his mirth, said to him,

"My dear sir, I do not see that you have the slightest right to demand satisfaction, since this gentleman confesses, like you, that he might have been mistaken."

"But," remarked the officer, "is it credible that he was at the battle of Arbela?"

"This gentleman leaves you free to believe or not to believe, and he is at liberty to assert that he was there until you can prove the contrary. Do you wish to deny it to make him draw his sword?"

"God forbid! I would rather consider the affair ended."

"Well, gentlemen," said the commander, "I have but one more duty to perform, and it is to advise you to embrace one another like two honest men."

We followed the advice with great pleasure.

The next day, the Provencal, rather crestfallen, came to share my dinner, and I gave him a friendly welcome. Thus was ended that comic adventure, to the great satisfaction of M. de la Haye.

IV

I Receive Good News From Venice, to Which City I Return with De la Haye and Bavois—My Three Friends Give Me a Warm Welcome; Their Surprise at Finding Me a Model of Devotion—Bavois Lures Me Back to My Former Way of Living—De la Haye a Thorough Hypocrite—Adventure with the Girl Marchetti—I Win a Prize in the Lottery—I Meet Baletti—De la Haye Leaves M. de Bragadin's Palace—My Departure for Paris.

Whilst De la Haye was every day gaining greater influence over my weakened mind, whilst I was every day devoutly attending mass, sermons, and every office of the Church, I received from Venice a letter containing the pleasant information that my affair had followed its natural course, namely, that it was entirely forgotten; and in another letter M. de Bragadin informed me that the minister had written to the Venetian ambassador in Rome with instructions to assure the Holy Father that Baron Bavois would, immediately after his arrival in Venice, receive in the army of the Republic an appointment which would enable him to live honourably and to gain a high position by his talents.

That letter overcame M. de la Haye with joy, and I completed his happiness by telling him that nothing hindered me from going back to my native city.

He immediately made up his mind to go to Modena in order to explain to his pupil how he was to act in Venice to open for himself the way to a brilliant fortune. De la Haye depended on me in every way; he saw my fanaticism, and he was well aware that it is a disease which rages as long as the causes from which it has sprung are in existence. As he was going with me to Venice, he flattered himself that he could easily feed the fire he had lighted. Therefore he wrote to Bavois that he would join him immediately, and two days after he took leave of me, weeping abundantly, praising highly the virtues of my soul, calling me his son, his dear son, and assuring me that his great affection for me had been caused by the mark of election which he had seen on my countenance. After that, I felt my calling and election were sure.

A few days after the departure of De la Haye, I left Parma in my carriage with which I parted in Fusina, and from there I proceeded to Venice. After an absence of a year, my three friends received me as if I had been their guardian angel. They expressed their impatience to welcome the two saints announced by my letters. An apartment was ready for De la Haye in the palace of M. de Bragadin, and as state reasons did not allow my father to receive in his own house a foreigner who had not yet entered the service of the Republic, two rooms had been engaged for Bavois in the neighbourhood.

They were thoroughly amazed at the wonderful change which had taken place in my morals. Every day attending mass, often present at the preaching and at the other services, never shewing myself at the casino, frequenting only a certain cafe which was the place of meeting for all men of acknowledged piety and reserve, and always studying when I was not in their company. When they compared my actual mode of living with the former one, they marvelled, and they could not sufficiently thank the eternal providence of God whose inconceivable ways they admired. They blessed the criminal actions which had compelled me to remain one year away from my native place. I crowned their delight by paying all my debts without asking any money from M. de Bragadin, who, not having given me anything for one year, had religiously put together every month the sum he had allowed me. I need not say how pleased the worthy friends were, when they saw that I had entirely given up gambling.

I had a letter from De la Haye in the beginning of May. He announced that he was on the eve of starting with the son so dear to his heart, and that he would soon place himself at the disposition of the respectable men to whom I had announced him.

Knowing the hour at which the barge arrived from Modena, we all went to meet them, except M. de Bragadin, who was engaged at the senate. We returned to the palace before him, and when he came back, finding us all together, he gave his new guests the most friendly welcome. De la Haye spoke to me of a hundred things, but I scarcely heard what he said, so much was my attention taken up by Bavois. He was so different to what I had fancied him to be from the impression I had received from De la Haye, that my ideas were altogether upset. I had to study him; for three days before I could make up my mind to like him. I must give his portrait to my readers.

Baron Bavois was a young man of about twenty-five, of middle size, handsome in features, well made, fair, of an equable temper, speaking well and with intelligence, and uttering his words with a tone of modesty which suited him exactly. His features were regular and pleasing, his teeth were beautiful, his hair was long and fine, always well taken care of, and exhaling the perfume of the pomatum with which it was dressed. That individual, who was the exact opposite of the man that De la Haye had led me to imagine, surprised my friends greatly, but their welcome did not in any way betray their astonishment, for their pure and candid minds would not admit a judgment contrary to the good opinion they had formed of his morals. As soon as we had established De la Haye in his beautiful apartment, I accompanied Bavois to the rooms engaged for him, where his luggage had been sent by my orders. He found himself in very comfortable quarters, and being received with distinction by his worthy host, who was already greatly prejudiced in his favour, the young baron embraced me warmly, pouring out all his gratitude, and assuring me that he felt deeply all I had done for him without knowing him, as De la Haye had informed him of all that had occurred. I pretended not to understand what he was alluding to, and to change the subject of conversation I asked him how he intended to occupy his time in Venice until his military appointment gave him serious duties to perform. "I trust," he answered, "that we shall enjoy ourselves in an agreeable way, for I have no doubt that our inclinations are the same."

Mercury and De la Haye had so completely besotted me that I should have found some difficulty in understanding these words, however intelligible they were; but if I did not go any further than the outward signification of his answer, I could not help remarking that he had already taken the fancy of the two daughters of the house. They were neither pretty nor ugly, but he shewed himself gracious towards them like a man who understands his business. I had, however, already made such great progress in my mystical education, that I considered the compliments he addressed to the girls as mere forms of politeness.

For the first day, I took my young baron only to the St. Mark's Square and to the cafe, where we remained until supper-time, as it had been arranged that he would take his meals with us. At the supper-table he shewed himself very witty, and M. Dandolo named an hour for the next day, when he intended to present him to the secretary for war. In the evening I accompanied him to his lodging, where I found that the two young girls were delighted because the young Swiss nobleman had no servant, and because they hoped to convince him that he would not require one.

The next day, a little earlier than the time appointed, I called upon him with M. Dandolo and M. Barbaro, who were both to present him at the war office. We found him at his toilet under the delicate hands of the eldest girl, who was dressing his hair. His room, was fragrant with the perfumes of his pomatums and scents. This did not indicate a sainted man; yet my two friends did not feel scandalized, although their astonishment was very evident, for they had not expected that show of gallantry from a young neophyte. I was nearly bursting into a loud laugh, when I heard M. Dandolo remark that, unless we hurried, we would not have time to hear mass, whereupon Bavois enquired whether it was a festival. M. Dandolo, without passing any remark, answered negatively, and after that, mass was not again mentioned. When Bavois was ready, I left them and went a different way. I met them again at dinner-time, during which the reception given to the young baron by the secretary was discussed, and in the evening my friends introduced him to several ladies who were much pleased with him. In less than a week he was so well known that there was no fear of his time hanging wearily on his hands, but that week was likewise enough to give me a perfect insight into his nature and way of thinking. I should not have required such a long study, if I had not at first begun on a wrong scent, or rather if my intelligence had not been stultified by my fanaticism. Bavois was particularly fond of women, of gambling, of every luxury, and, as he was poor, women supplied him with the best part of his resources. As to religious faith he had none, and as he was no hypocrite he confessed as much to me.

"How have you contrived," I said to him one day, "such as you are, to deceive De la Haye?"

"God forbid I should deceive anyone. De la Haye is perfectly well aware of my system, and of my way of thinking on religious matters, but, being himself very devout, he entertains a holy sympathy for my soul, and I do not object to it. He has bestowed many kindnesses upon me, and I feel grateful to him; my affection for him is all the greater because he never teases me with his dogmatic lessons or with sermons respecting my salvation, of which I have no doubt that God, in His fatherly goodness, will take care. All this is settled between De la Haye and me, and we live on the best of terms."

The best part of the joke is that, while I was studying him, Bavois, without knowing it, restored my mind to its original state, and I was ashamed of myself when I realized that I had been the dupe of a Jesuit who was an arrant hypocrite, in spite of the character of holiness which he assumed, and which he could play with such marvellous ability. From that moment I fell again into all my former practices. But let us return to De la Haye.

That late Jesuit, who in his inmost heart loved nothing but his own comfort, already advanced in years, and therefore no longer caring for the fair sex, was exactly the sort of man to please my simpleminded trio of friends. As he never spoke to them but of God, of His angels, and of everlasting glory, and as he was always accompanying them to church, they found him a delightful companion. They longed for the time when he would discover himself, for they imagined he was at the very least a Rosicrucian, or perhaps the hermit of Courpegna, who had taught me the cabalistic science and made me a present of the immortal Paralis. They felt grieved because the oracle had forbidden them, through my cabalistic lips, ever to mention my science in the presence of Tartufe.

As I had foreseen, that interdiction left me to enjoy as I pleased all the time that I would have been called upon to devote to their devout credulity, and besides, I was naturally afraid lest De la Haye, such as I truly believed him to be, would never lend himself to that trifling nonsense, and would, for the sake of deserving greater favour at their hands, endeavour to undeceive them and to take my place in their confidence.

I soon found out that I had acted with prudence, for in less than three weeks the cunning fox had obtained so great an influence over the mind of my three friends that he was foolish enough, not only to believe that he did not want me any more to support his credit with them, but likewise that he could supplant me whenever he chose. I could see it clearly in his way of addressing me, as well as in the change in his proceedings.

He was beginning to hold with my friends frequent conversations to which I was not summoned, and he had contrived to make them introduce him to several families which I was not in the habit of visiting. He assumed his grand jesuitic airs, and, although with honeyed word he would take the liberty of censuring me because I sometimes spent a night out, and, as he would say, "God knows where!"

I was particularly vexed at his seeming to accuse me of leading his pupil astray. He then would assume the tone of a man speaking jestingly, but I was not deceived. I thought it was time to put an end to his game, and with that intention I paid him a visit in his bedroom. When I was seated, I said,

"I come, as a true worshipper of the Gospel, to tell you in private something that, another time, I would say in public."

"What is it, my dear friend?"

"I advise you for the future not to hurl at me the slightest taunt respecting the life I am leading with Bavois, when we are in the presence of my three worthy friends. I do not object to listen to you when we are alone."

"You are wrong in taking my innocent jests seriously."

"Wrong or right, that does not matter. Why do you never attack your proselyte? Be careful for the future, or I might on my side, and only in jest like you, throw at your head some repartee which you have every reason to fear, and thus repay you with interest."

And bowing to him I left his room.

A few days afterwards I spent a few hours with my friends and Paralis, and the oracle enjoined them never to accomplish without my advice anything that might be recommended or even insinuated by Valentine; that was the cabalistic name of the disciple of Escobar. I knew I could rely upon their obedience to that order.

De la Haye soon took notice of some slight change; he became more reserved, and Bavois, whom I informed of what I had done, gave me his full approbation. He felt convinced, as I was, that De la Haye had been useful to him only through weak or selfish reasons, that is, that he would have cared little for his soul if his face had not been handsome, and if he had not known that he would derive important advantages from having caused his so-called conversion.

Finding that the Venetian government was postponing his appointment from day to day, Bavois entered the service of the French ambassador. The decision made it necessary for him not only to cease his visits to M. de Bragadin, but even to give up his intercourse with De la Haye, who was the guest of that senator.

It is one of the strictest laws of the Republic that the patricians and their families shall not hold any intercourse with the foreign ambassadors and their suites. But the decision taken by Bavois did not prevent my friends speaking in his favour, and they succeeded in obtaining employment for him, as will be seen further on.

The husband of Christine, whom I never visited, invited me to go to the casino which he was in the habit of frequenting with his aunt and his wife, who had already presented him with a token of their mutual affection. I accepted his invitation, and I found Christine as lovely as ever, and speaking the Venetian dialect like her husband. I made in that casino the acquaintance of a chemist, who inspired me with the wish to follow a course of chemistry. I went to his house, where I found a young girl who greatly pleased me. She was a neighbour, and came every evening to keep the chemist's elderly wife company, and at a regular hour a servant called to take her home. I had never made love to her but once in a trifling sort of way, and in the presence of the old lady, but I was surprised not to see her after that for several days, and I expressed my astonishment. The good lady told me that very likely the girl's cousin, an abbe, with whom she was residing, had heard of my seeing her every evening, had become jealous, and would not allow her to come again.

"An abbe jealous?"

"Why not? He never allows her to go out except on Sundays to attend the first mass at the Church of Santa Maria Mater Domini, close by his dwelling. He did not object to her coming here, because he knew that we never had any visitors, and very likely he has heard through the servant of your being here every evening."

A great enemy to all jealous persons, and a greater friend to my amorous fancies, I wrote to the young girl that, if she would leave her cousin for me, I would give her a house in which she should be the mistress, and that I would surround her with good society and with every luxury to be found in Venice. I added that I would be in the church on the following Sunday to receive her answer.

I did not forget my appointment, and her answer was that the abbe being her tyrant, she would consider herself happy to escape out of his clutches, but that she could not make up her mind to follow me unless I consented to marry her. She concluded her letter by saying that, in case I entertained honest intentions towards her, I had only to speak to her mother, Jeanne Marchetti, who resided in Lusia, a city thirty miles distant from Venice.

This letter piqued my curiosity, and I even imagined that she had written it in concert with the abbe. Thinking that they wanted to dupe me, and besides, finding the proposal of marriage ridiculous, I determined on having my revenge. But I wanted to get to the bottom of it, and I made up my mind to see the girl's mother. She felt honoured by my visit, and greatly pleased when, after I had shewn her her daughter's letter, I told her that I wished to marry her, but that I should never think of it as long as she resided with the abbe.

"That abbe," she said, "is a distant relative. He used to live alone in his house in Venice, and two years ago he told me that he was in want of a housekeeper. He asked me to let my daughter go to him in that capacity, assuring me that in Venice she would have good opportunities of getting married. He offered to give me a deed in writing stating that, on the day of her marriage, he would give her all his furniture valued at about one thousand ducats, and the inheritance of a small estate, bringing one hundred ducats a year, which he possesses here. It seemed to me a good bargain, and, my daughter being pleased with the offer, I accepted. He gave me the deed duly drawn by a notary, and my daughter went with him. I know that he makes a regular slave of her, but she chose to go. Nevertheless, I need not tell you that my most ardent wish is to see her married, for, as long as a girl is without a husband, she is too much exposed to temptation, and the poor mother cannot rest in peace."

"Then come to Venice with me. You will take your daughter out of the abbe's house, and I will make her my wife. Unless that is done I cannot marry her, for I should dishonour myself if I received my wife from his hands."

"Oh, no! for he is my cousin, although only in the fourth degree, and, what is more, he is a priest and says the mass every day."

"You make me laugh, my good woman. Everybody knows that a priest says the mass without depriving himself of certain trifling enjoyments. Take your daughter with you, or give up all hope of ever seeing her married."

"But if I take her with me, he will not give her his furniture, and perhaps he will sell his small estate here."

"I undertake to look to that part of the business. I promise to take her out of his hands, and to make her come back to you with all the furniture, and to obtain the estate when she is my wife. If you knew me better, you would not doubt what I say. Come to Venice, and I assure you that you shall return here in four or five days with your daughter."

She read the letter which had been written to me by her daughter again, and told me that, being a poor widow, she had not the money necessary to pay the expenses of her journey to Venice, or of her return to Louisa.

"In Venice you shall not want for anything," I said; "in the mean time, here are ten sequins."

"Ten sequins! Then I can go with my sister-in-law?"

"Come with anyone you like, but let us go soon so as to reach Chiozza, where we must sleep. To-morrow we shall dine in Venice, and I undertake to defray all expenses."

We arrived in Venice the next day at ten o'clock, and I took the two women to Castello, to a house the first floor of which was empty. I left them there, and provided with the deed signed by the abbe I went to dine with my three friends, to whom I said that I had been to Chiozza on important business. After dinner, I called upon the lawyer, Marco de Lesse, who told me that if the mother presented a petition to the President of the Council of Ten, she would immediately be invested with power to take her daughter away with all the furniture in the house, which she could send wherever she pleased. I instructed him to have the petition ready, saying that I would come the next morning with the mother, who would sign it in his presence.

I brought the mother early in the morning, and after she had signed the petition we went to the Boussole, where she presented it to the President of the Council. In less than a quarter of an hour a bailiff was ordered to repair to the house of the priest with the mother, and to put her in possession of her daughter, and of all the furniture, which she would immediately take away.

The order was carried into execution to the very letter. I was with the mother in a gondola as near as possible to the house, and I had provided a large boat in which the sbirri stowed all the furniture found on the premises. When it was all done, the daughter was brought to the gondola, and she was extremely surprised to see me. Her mother kissed her, and told her that I would be her husband the very next day. She answered that she was delighted, and that nothing had been left in her tyrant's house except his bed and his clothes.

When we reached Castello, I ordered the furniture to be brought out of the boat; we had dinner, and I told the three women that they must go back to Lusia, where I would join them as soon as I had settled all my affairs. I spent the afternoon gaily with my intended. She told us that the abbe was dressing when the bailiff presented the order of the Council of Ten, with injunctions to allow its free execution under penalty of death; that the abbe finished his toilet, went out to say his mass, and that everything had been done without the slightest opposition. "I was told," she added, "that my mother was waiting for me in the gondola, but I did not expect to find you, and I never suspected that you were at the bottom of the whole affair."

"It is the first proof I give you of my love."

These words made her smile very pleasantly.

I took care to have a good supper and some excellent wines, and after we had spent two hours at table in the midst of the joys of Bacchus, I devoted four more to a pleasant tete-a-tete with my intended bride.

The next morning, after breakfast, I had the whole of the furniture stowed in a peotta, which I had engaged for the purpose and paid for beforehand. I gave ten more sequins to the mother, and sent them away all three in great delight. The affair was completed to my honour as well as to my entire satisfaction, and I returned home.

The case had made so much noise that my friends could not have remained ignorant of it; the consequence was that, when they saw me, they shewed their surprise and sorrow. De la Haye embraced me with an air of profound grief, but it was a feigned feeling—a harlequin's dress, which he had the talent of assuming with the greatest facility. M. de Bragadin alone laughed heartily, saying to the others that they did not understand the affair, and that it was the forerunner of something great which was known only to heavenly spirits. On my side, being ignorant of the opinion they entertained of the matter, and certain that they were not informed of all the circumstances, I laughed like M. de Bragadin, but said nothing. I had nothing to fear, and I wanted to amuse myself with all that would be said.

We sat down to table, and M. Barbaro was the first to tell me in a friendly manner that he hoped at least that this was not the day after my wedding.

"Then people say that I am married?"

"It is said everywhere and by everybody. The members of the Council themselves believe it, and they have good reason to believe that they are right."

"To be right in believing such a thing, they ought to be certain of it, and those gentlemen have no such certainty. As they are not infallible any more than any one, except God, I tell you that they are mistaken. I like to perform good actions and to get pleasure for my money, but not at the expense of my liberty: Whenever you want to know my affairs, recollect that you can receive information about them only from me, and public rumour is only good to amuse fools."

"But," said M. Dandolo, "you spent the night with the person who is represented as your wife?"

"Quite true, but I have no account to give to anyone respecting what I have done last night. Are you not of my opinion, M. de la Haye?"

"I wish you would not ask my opinion, for I do not know. But I must say that public rumour ought not to be despised. The deep affection I have for you causes me to grieve for what the public voice says about you."

"How is it that those reports do not grieve M. de Bragadin, who has certainly greater affection for me than you have?"

"I respect you, but I have learned at my own expense that slander is to be feared. It is said that, in order to get hold of a young girl who was residing with her uncle—a worthy priest, you suborned a woman who declared herself to be the girl's mother, and thus deceived the Supreme Council, through the authority of which she obtained possession of the girl for you. The bailiff sent by the Council swears that you were in the gondola with the false mother when the young girl joined her. It is said that the deed, in virtue of which you caused the worthy ecclesiastic's furniture to be carried off, is false, and you are blamed for having made the highest body of the State a stepping-stone to crime. In fine, it is said that, even if you have married the girl, and no doubt of it is entertained, the members of the Council will not be silent as to the fraudulent means you have had recourse to in order to carry out your intentions successfully."

"That is a very long speech," I said to him, coldly, "but learn from me that a wise man who has heard a criminal accusation related with so many absurd particulars ceases to be wise when he makes himself the echo of what he has heard, for if the accusation should turn out to be a calumny, he would himself become the accomplice of the slanderer."

After that sentence, which brought the blood to the face of the Jesuit, but which my friends thought very wise, I entreated him, in a meaning voice, to spare his anxiety about me, and to be quite certain that I knew the laws of honour, and that I had judgment enough to take care of myself, and to let foul tongues say what they liked about me, just as I did when I heard them speak ill of him.

The adventure was the talk of the city for five or six days, after which it was soon forgotten.

But three months having elapsed without my having paid any visit to Lusia, or having answered the letters written to me by the damigella

Marchetti, and without sending her the money she claimed of me, she made up her mind to take certain proceedings which might have had serious consequences, although they had none whatever in the end.

One day, Ignacio, the bailiff of the dreaded tribunal of the State inquisitors, presented himself as I was sitting at table with my friends, De la Haye, and two other guests. He informed me that the Cavaliere Cantarini dal Zoffo wished to see me, and would wait for me the next morning at such an hour at the Madonna de l'Orto. I rose from the table and answered, with a bow, that I would not fail to obey the wishes of his excellency. The bailiff then left us.

I could not possibly guess what such a high dignitary of State could want with my humble person, yet the message made us rather anxious, for Cantarini dal Zoffo was one of the Inquisitors, that is to say, a bird of very ill omen. M. de Bragadin, who had been Inquisitor while he was Councillor, and therefore knew the habits of the tribunal, told me that I had nothing to fear.

"Ignacio was dressed in private clothes," he added, "and therefore he did not come as the official messenger of the dread tribunal. M. Cantarini wishes to speak to you only as a private citizen, as he sends you word to call at his palace and not at the court-house. He is an elderly man, strict but just, to whom you must speak frankly and without equivocating, otherwise you would make matters worse."

I was pleased with M. de Bragadin's advice, which was of great use to me. I called at the appointed time.

I was immediately announced, and I had not long to wait. I entered the room, and his excellency, seated at a table, examined me from head to foot for one minute without speaking to me; he then rang the bell, and ordered his servant to introduce the two ladies who were waiting in the next room. I guessed at once what was the matter, and felt no surprise when I saw the woman Marchetti and her daughter. His excellency asked me if I knew them.

"I must know them, monsignor, as one of them will become my wife when she has convinced me by her good conduct that she is worthy of that honour."

"Her conduct is good, she lives with her mother at Lusia; you have deceived her. Why do you postpone your marriage with her? Why do you not visit her? You never answer her letters, and you let her be in want."

"I cannot marry her, your excellency, before I have enough to support her. That will come in three or four years, thanks to a situation which M.

de Bragadin, my only protector, promises to obtain for me. Until then she must live honestly, and support herself by working. I will only marry her when I am convinced of her honesty, and particularly when I am certain that she has given up all intercourse with the abbe, her cousin in the fourth degree. I do not visit her because my confessor and my conscience forbid me to go to her house."

"She wishes you to give her a legal promise of marriage, and sustentation."

"Monsignor, I am under no obligation to give her a promise of marriage, and having no means whatever I cannot support her. She must earn her own living with her mother."

"When she lived with her cousin," said her mother, "she never wanted anything, and she shall go back to him."

"If she returns to his house I shall not take the trouble of taking her out of his hands a second time, and your excellency will then see that I was right to defer my marriage with her until I was convinced of her honesty."

The judge told me that my presence, was no longer necessary. It was the end of the affair, and I never heard any more about it. The recital of the dialogue greatly amused my friends.

At the beginning of the Carnival of 1750 I won a prize of three thousand ducats at the lottery. Fortune made me that present when I did not require it, for I had held the bank during the autumn, and had won. It was at a casino where no nobleman dared to present himself, because one of the partners was an officer in the service of the Duke de Montalegre, the Spanish Ambassador. The citizens of Venice felt ill at ease with the patricians, and that is always the case under an aristocratic government, because equality exists in reality only between the members of such a government.

As I intended to take a trip to Paris, I placed one thousand sequins in M. de Bragadin's hands, and with that project in view I had the courage to pass the carnival without risking my money at the faro-table. I had taken a share of one-fourth in the bank of an honest patrician, and early in Lent he handed me a large sum.

Towards mid-Lent my friend Baletti returned from Mantua to Venice. He was engaged at the St. Moses Theatre as ballet-master during the Fair of the Assumption. He was with Marina, but they did not live together. She made the conquest of an English Jew, called Mendez, who spent a great deal of money for her. That Jew gave me good news of Therese, whom he had known in Naples, and in whose hands he had left some of his spoils. The information pleased me, and I was very glad to have been prevented by Henriette from joining Therese in Naples, as I had intended, for I should certainly have fallen in love with her again, and God knows what the consequences might have been.

It was at that time that Bavois was appointed captain in the service of the Republic; he rose rapidly in his profession, as I shall mention hereafter.

De la Haye undertook the education of a young nobleman called Felix Calvi, and a short time afterwards he accompanied him to Poland. I met him again in Vienna three years later.

I was making my preparations to go to the Fair of Reggio, then to Turin, where the whole of Italy was congregating for the marriage of the Duke of Savoy with a princess of Spain, daughter of Philip V, and lastly to Paris, where, Madame la Dauphine being pregnant, magnificent preparations were made in the expectation of the birth of a prince. Baletti was likewise on the point of undertaking the same journey. He was recalled by his parents, who were dramatic artists: his mother was the celebrated Silvia.

Baletti was engaged at the Italian Theatre in Paris as dancer and first gentleman. I could not choose a companion more to my taste, more agreeable, or in a better position to procure me numerous advantageous acquaintances in Paris.

I bade farewell to my three excellent friends, promising to return within two years.

I left my brother Francois in the studio of Simonetti, the painter of battle pieces, known as the Parmesan. I gave him a promise to think of him in Paris, where, at that time particularly, great talent was always certain of a high fortune. My readers will see how I kept my word.

I likewise left in Venice my brother Jean, who had returned to that city after having travelled through Italy with Guarienti. He was on the point of going to Rome, where he remained fourteen years in the studio of Raphael Mengs. He left Rome for Dresden in 1764, where he died in the year 1795.

Baletti started before me, and I left Venice, to meet him in Reggio, on the 1st of June, 1750. I was well fitted out, well supplied with money, and sure not to want for any, if I led a proper life. We shall soon see, dear reader, what judgment you will pass on my conduct, or rather I shall not see it, for I know that when you are able to judge, I shall no longer care for your sentence.

V

I Stop at Ferrara, Where I Have a Comic Adventure—My Arrival in Paris.

Precisely at twelve o'clock the peotta landed me at Ponte di Lago Oscuro, and I immediately took a post-chaise to reach Ferrara in time for dinner. I put up at St. Mark's Hotel. I was following the waiter up the stairs, when a joyful uproar, which suddenly burst from a room the door of which was open, made me curious to ascertain the cause of so much mirth. I peeped into the room, and saw some twelve persons, men and women, seated round a well-supplied table. It was a very natural thing, and I was moving on, when I was stopped by the exclamation, "Ah, here he is!" uttered by the pretty voice of a woman, and at the same moment, the speaker, leaving the table, came to me with open arms and embraced me, saying,

"Quick, quick, a seat for him near me; take his luggage to his room."

A young man came up, and she said to him, "Well, I told you he would arrive to-day?"

She made me sit near her at the table, after I had been saluted by all the guests who had risen to do me honour.

"My dear cousin," she said, addressing me, "you must be hungry;" and as she spoke she squeezed my foot under the table. "Here is my intended husband whom I beg to introduce to you, as well as my father and mother-in-law. The other guests round the table are friends of the family. But, my dear cousin, tell me why my mother has not come with you?"

At last I had to open my lips!

"Your mother, my dear cousin, will be here in three or four days, at the latest."

I thought that my newly-found cousin was unknown to me, but when I looked at her with more attention, I fancied I recollected her features. She was the Catinella, a dancer of reputation, but I had never spoken to her before. I easily guessed that she was giving me an impromptu part in a play of her own composition, and I was to be a 'deux ex machina'. Whatever is singular and unexpected has always attracted me, and as my cousin was pretty, I lent myself most willingly to the joke, entertaining no doubt that she would reward me in an agreeable manner. All I had to do was to play my part well, but without implicating myself. Therefore, pretending to be very hungry, I gave her the opportunity of speaking and of informing me by hints of what I had to know, in order not to make blunders. Understanding the reason of my reserve, she afforded me the proof of her quick intelligence by saying sometimes to one person, sometimes to the other, everything it was necessary for me to know. Thus I learnt that the wedding could not take place until the arrival of her mother, who was to bring the wardrobe and the diamonds of my cousin. I was the precentor going to Turin to compose the music of the opera which was to be represented at the marriage of the Duke of Savoy. This last discovery pleased me greatly, because I saw that I should have no difficulty in taking my departure the next morning, and I began to enjoy the part I had to play. Yet, if I had not reckoned upon the reward, I might very well have informed the honourable company that my false cousin was mad, but, although Catinella was very near thirty, she was very pretty and celebrated for her intrigues; that was enough, and she could turn me round her little finger.

The future mother-in-law was seated opposite, and to do me honour she filled a glass and offered it to me. Already identified with my part in the comedy, I put forth my hand to take the glass, but seeing that my hand was somewhat bent, she said to me,

"What is the matter with your hand, sir?"

"Nothing serious, madam; only a slight sprain which a little rest will soon cure."

At these words, Catinella, laughing heartily, said that she regretted the accident because it would deprive her friends of the pleasure they would have enjoyed in hearing me play the harpsichord.

"I am glad to find it a laughing matter, cousin."

"I laugh, because it reminds me of a sprained ankle which I once feigned to have in order not to dance."

After coffee, the mother-in-law, who evidently understood what was proper, said that most likely my cousin wanted to talk with me on family matters, and that we ought to be left alone.

Every one of the guests left the room.

As soon as I was alone with her in my room, which was next to her own she threw herself on a sofa, and gave way to a most immoderate fit of laughter.

"Although I only know you by name," she said to me, "I have entire confidence in you, but you will do well to go away to-morrow. I have been here for two months without any money. I have nothing but a few dresses and some linen, which I should have been compelled to sell to defray my expenses if I had not been lucky enough to inspire the son of the landlord with the deepest love. I have flattered his passion by promising to become his wife, and to bring him as a marriage portion twenty thousand crowns' worth of diamonds which I am supposed to have in Venice, and which my mother is expected to bring with her. But my mother has nothing and knows nothing of the affair, therefore she is not likely to leave Venice."

"But, tell me, lovely madcap, what will be the end of this extravaganza? I am afraid it will take a tragic turn at the last."

"You are mistaken; it will remain a comedy, and a very amusing one, too. I am expecting every hour the arrival of Count Holstein, brother of the Elector of Mainz. He has written to me from Frankfort; he has left that city, and must by this time have reached Venice. He will take me to the Fair of Reggio, and if my intended takes it into his head to be angry, the count will thrash him and pay my bill, but I am determined that he shall be neither thrashed nor paid. As I go away, I have only to whisper in his ear that I will certainly return, and it will be all right. I know my promise to become his wife as soon as I come back will make him happy."

"That's all very well! You are as witty as a cousin of Satan, but I shall not wait your return to marry you; our wedding must take place at once."

"What folly! Well, wait until this evening."

"Not a bit of it, for I can almost fancy I hear the count's carriage. If he should not arrive, we can continue the sport during the night."

"Do you love me?"

"To distraction! but what does it matter? However, your excellent comedy renders you worthy of adoration. Now, suppose we do not waste our time."

"You are right: it is an episode, and all the more agreeable for being impromptu."

I can well recollect that I found it a delightful episode. Towards evening all the family joined us again, a walk was proposed, and we were on the point of going out, when a carriage drawn by six post-horses noisily entered the yard. Catinella looked through the window, and desired to be left alone, saying that it was a prince who had come to see her. Everybody went away, she pushed me into my room and locked me in. I went to the window, and saw a nobleman four times as big as myself getting out of the carriage. He came upstairs, entered the room of the intended bride, and all that was left to me was the consolation of having seized fortune by the forelock, the pleasure of hearing their conversation, and a convenient view, through a crevice in the partition, of what Catinella contrived to do with that heavy lump of flesh. But at last the stupid amusement wearied me, for it lasted five hours, which were employed in amorous caresses, in packing Catinella's rags, in loading them on the carriage, in taking supper, and in drinking numerous bumpers of Rhenish wine. At midnight the count left the hotel, carrying away with him the beloved mistress of the landlord's son.

No one during those long hours had come to my room, and I had not called. I was afraid of being discovered, and I did not know how far the German prince would have been pleased if he had found out that he had an indiscreet witness of the heavy and powerless demonstrations of his tenderness, which were a credit to neither of the actors, and which supplied me with ample food for thoughts upon the miseries of mankind.

After the departure of the heroine, catching through the crevice a glimpse of the abandoned lover, I called out to him to unlock my door. The poor silly fellow told me piteously that, Catinella having taken the key with her, it would be necessary to break the door open. I begged him to have it done at once, because I was hungry. As soon as I was out of my prison I had my supper, and the unfortunate lover kept me company. He told me that Catinella had found a moment to promise him that she would return within six weeks, that she was shedding tears in giving him that assurance, and that she had kissed him with great tenderness.

"Has the prince paid her expenses?"

"Not at all. We would not have allowed him to do it, even if he had offered. My future wife would have felt offended, for you can have no idea of the delicacy of her feelings."

"What does your father say of her departure?"

"My father always sees the worst side of everything; he says that she will never come back, and my mother shares his opinion rather than mine. But you, signor maestro, what do you think?"

"That if she has promised to return, she will be sure to keep her word."

"Of course; for if she did not mean to come back, she would not have given me her promise."

"Precisely; I call that a good argument."

I had for my supper what was left of the meal prepared by the count's cook, and I drank a bottle of excellent Rhenish wine which Catinella had juggled away to treat her intended husband, and which the worthy fellow thought could not have a better destination than to treat his future cousin. After supper I took post-horses and continued my journey, assuring the unhappy, forlorn lover that I would do all I could to persuade my cousin to come back very soon. I wanted to pay my bill, but he refused to receive any money. I reached Bologna a few minutes after Catinella, and put up at the same hotel, where I found an opportunity of telling her all her lover had said. I arrived in Reggio before her, but I could not speak to her in that city, for she was always in the company of her potent and impotent lord. After the fair, during which nothing of importance occurred to me, I left Reggio with my friend Baletti and we proceeded to Turin, which I wanted to see, for the first time I had gone to that city with Henriette I had stopped only long enough to change horses.

I found everything beautiful in Turin, the city, the court, the theatre, and the women, including the Duchess of Savoy, but I could not help laughing when I was told that the police of the city was very efficient, for the streets were full of beggars. That police, however, was the special care of the king, who was very intelligent; if we are to believe history, but I confess that I laughed when I saw the ridiculous face of that sovereign.

I had never seen a king before in my life, and a foolish idea made me suppose that a king must be preeminent—a very rare being—by his beauty and the majesty of his appearance, and in everything superior to the rest of men. For a young Republican endowed with reason, my idea was not, after all, so very foolish, but I very soon got rid of it when I saw that King of Sardinia, ugly, hump-backed, morose and vulgar even in his manners. I then realized that it was possible to be a king without being entirely a man.

I saw L'Astrua and Gafarello, those two magnificent singers on the stage, and I admired the dancing of La Geofroi, who married at that time a worthy dancer named Bodin.

During my stay in Turin, no amorous fancy disturbed the peace of my soul, except an accident which happened to me with the daughter of my washerwoman, and which increased my knowledge in physics in a singular manner. That girl was very pretty, and, without being what might be called in love with her, I wished to obtain her favours. Piqued at my not being able to obtain an appointment from her, I contrived one day to catch her at the bottom of a back staircase by which she used to come to my room, and, I must confess, with the intention of using a little violence, if necessary.

Having concealed myself for that purpose at the time I expected her, I got hold of her by surprise, and, half by persuasion, half by the rapidity of my attack, she was brought to a right position, and I lost no time in engaging in action. But at the first movement of the connection a loud explosion somewhat cooled my ardour, the more so that the young girl covered her face with her hands as if she wished to hide her shame. However, encouraging her with a loving kiss, I began again. But, a report, louder even than the first, strikes at the same moment my ear and my nose. I continue; a third, a fourth report, and, to make a long matter short, each movement gives an explosion with as much regularity as a conductor making the time for a piece of music!

This extraordinary phenomenon, the confusion of the poor girl, our position—everything, in fact, struck me as so comical, that I burst into the most immoderate laughter, which compelled me to give up the undertaking. Ashamed and confused, the young girl ran away, and I did nothing to hinder her. After that she never had the courage to present herself before me. I remained seated on the stairs for a quarter of an hour after she had left me, amused at the funny character of a scene which even now excites my mirth. I suppose that the young girl was indebted for her virtue to that singular disease, and most likely, if it were common to all the fair sex, there would be fewer gallant women, unless we had different organs; for to pay for one moment of enjoyment at the expense both of the hearing and of the smell is to give too high a price.

Baletti, being in a hurry to reach Paris, where great preparations were being made for the birth of a Duke of Burgundy—for the duchess was near the time of her delivery—easily persuaded me to shorten my stay in Turin. We therefore left that city, and in five days we arrived at Lyons, where I stayed about a week.

Lyons is a very fine city in which at that time there were scarcely three or four noble houses opened to strangers; but, in compensation, there were more than a hundred hospitable ones belonging to merchants, manufacturers, and commission agents, amongst whom was to be found an excellent society remarkable for easy manners, politeness, frankness, and good style, without the absurd pride to be met with amongst the nobility in the provinces, with very few honourable exceptions. It is true that the standard of good manners is below that of Paris, but one soon gets accustomed to it. The wealth of Lyons arises from good taste and low prices, and Fashion is the goddess to whom that city owes its prosperity. Fashion alters every year, and the stuff, to which the fashion of the day gives a value equal, say to thirty, is the next year reduced to fifteen or twenty, and then it is sent to foreign countries where it is bought up as a novelty.

The manufacturers of Lyons give high salaries to designers of talent; in that lies the secret of their success. Low prices come from Competition—a fruitful source of wealth, and a daughter of Liberty. Therefore, a government wishing to establish on a firm basis the prosperity of trade must give commerce full liberty; only being careful to prevent the frauds which private interests, often wrongly understood, might invent at the expense of public and general interests. In fact, the government must hold the scales, and allow the citizens to load them as they please.

In Lyons I met the most famous courtezan of Venice. It was generally admitted that her equal had never been seen. Her name was Ancilla. Every man who saw her coveted her, and she was so kindly disposed that she could not refuse her favours to anyone; for if all men loved her one after the other, she returned the compliment by loving them all at once, and with her pecuniary advantages were only a very secondary consideration.

Venice has always been blessed with courtezans more celebrated by their beauty than their wit. Those who were most famous in my younger days were Ancilla and another called Spina, both the daughters of gondoliers, and both killed very young by the excesses of a profession which, in their eyes, was a noble one. At the age of twenty-two, Ancilla turned a dancer and Spina became a singer. Campioni, a celebrated Venetian dancer, imparted to the lovely Ancilla all the graces and the talents of which her physical perfections were susceptible, and married her. Spina had for her master a castrato who succeeded in making of her only a very ordinary singer, and in the absence of talent she was compelled, in order to get a living, to make the most of the beauty she had received from nature.

I shall have occasion to speak again of Ancilla before her death. She was then in Lyons with her husband; they had just returned from England, where they had been greatly applauded at the Haymarket Theatre. She had stopped in Lyons only for her pleasure, and, the moment she shewed herself, she had at her feet the most brilliant young men of the town, who were the slaves of her slightest caprice. Every day parties of pleasure, every evening magnificent suppers, and every night a great faro bank. The banker at the gaming table was a certain Don Joseph Marratti, the same man whom I had known in the Spanish army under the name of Don Pepe il Cadetto, and a few years afterwards assumed the name of Afflisio, and came to such a bad end. That faro bank won in a few days three hundred thousand francs. In a capital that would not have been considered a large sum, but in a commercial and industrial city like Lyons it raised the alarm amongst the merchants, and the Ultramontanes thought of taking their leave.

It was in Lyons that a respectable individual, whose acquaintance I made at the house of M. de Rochebaron, obtained for me the favour of being initiated in the sublime trifles of Freemasonry. I arrived in Paris a simple apprentice; a few months after my arrival I became companion and master; the last is certainly the highest degree in Freemasonry, for all the other degrees which I took afterwards are only pleasing inventions, which, although symbolical, add nothing to the dignity of master.

No one in this world can obtain a knowledge of everything, but every man who feels himself endowed with faculties, and can realize the extent of his moral strength, should endeavour to obtain the greatest possible amount of knowledge. A well-born young man who wishes to travel and know not only the world, but also what is called good society, who does not want to find himself, under certain circumstances, inferior to his equals, and excluded from participating in all their pleasures, must get himself initiated in what is called Freemasonry, even if it is only to know superficially what Freemasonry is. It is a charitable institution, which, at certain times and in certain places, may have been a pretext for criminal underplots got up for the overthrow of public order, but is there anything under heaven that has not been abused? Have we not seen the Jesuits, under the cloak of our holy religion, thrust into the parricidal hand of blind enthusiasts the dagger with which kings were to be assassinated! All men of importance, I mean those whose social existence is marked by intelligence and merit, by learning or by wealth, can be (and many of them are) Freemasons: is it possible to suppose that such meetings, in which the initiated, making it a law never to speak, 'intra muros', either of politics, or of religions, or of governments, converse only concerning emblems which are either moral or trifling; is it possible to suppose, I repeat, that those meetings, in which the governments may have their own creatures, can offer dangers sufficiently serious to warrant the proscriptions of kings or the excommunications of Popes?

In reality such proceedings miss the end for which they are undertaken, and the Pope, in spite of his infallibility, will not prevent his persecutions from giving Freemasonry an importance which it would perhaps have never obtained if it had been left alone. Mystery is the essence of man's nature, and whatever presents itself to mankind under a mysterious appearance will always excite curiosity and be sought, even when men are satisfied that the veil covers nothing but a cypher.

Upon the whole, I would advise all well-born young men, who intend to travel, to become Freemasons; but I would likewise advise them to be careful in selecting a lodge, because, although bad company cannot have any influence while inside of the lodge, the candidate must guard against bad acquaintances.

Those who become Freemasons only for the sake of finding out the secret of the order, run a very great risk of growing old under the trowel without ever realizing their purpose. Yet there is a secret, but it is so inviolable that it has never been confided or whispered to anyone. Those who stop at the outward crust of things imagine that the secret consists in words, in signs, or that the main point of it is to be found only in reaching the highest degree. This is a mistaken view: the man who guesses the secret of Freemasonry, and to know it you must guess it, reaches that point only through long attendance in the lodges, through deep thinking, comparison, and deduction. He would not trust that secret to his best friend in Freemasonry, because he is aware that if his friend has not found it out, he could not make any use of it after it had been whispered in his ear. No, he keeps his peace, and the secret remains a secret.

Everything done in a lodge must be secret; but those who have unscrupulously revealed what is done in the lodge, have been unable to reveal that which is essential; they had no knowledge of it, and had they known it, they certainly would not have unveiled the mystery of the ceremonies.

The impression felt in our days by the non-initiated is of the same nature as that felt in former times by those who were not initiated in the mysteries enacted at Eleusis in honour of Ceres. But the mysteries of Eleusis interested the whole of Greece, and whoever had attained some eminence in the society of those days had an ardent wish to take a part in those mysterious ceremonies, while Freemasonry, in the midst of many men of the highest merit, reckons a crowd of scoundrels whom no society ought to acknowledge, because they are the refuse of mankind as far as morality is concerned.

In the mysteries of Ceres, an inscrutable silence was long kept, owing to the veneration in which they were held. Besides, what was there in them that could be revealed? The three words which the hierophant said to the initiated? But what would that revelation have come to? Only to dishonour the indiscreet initiate, for they were barbarous words unknown to the vulgar. I have read somewhere that the three sacred words of the mysteries of Eleusis meant: Watch, and do no evil. The sacred words and the secrets of the various masonic degrees are about as criminal.

The initiation in the mysteries of Eleusis lasted nine days. The ceremonies were very imposing, and the company of the highest. Plutarch informs us that Alcibiades was sentenced to death and his property confiscated, because he had dared to turn the mysteries into ridicule in his house. He was even sentenced to be cursed by the priests and priestesses, but the curse was not pronounced because one of the priestesses opposed it, saying:

"I am a priestess to bless and not to curse!"

Sublime words! Lessons of wisdom and of morality which the Pope despises, but which the Gospel teaches and which the Saviour prescribes.

In our days nothing is important, and nothing is sacred, for our cosmopolitan philosophers.

Botarelli publishes in a pamphlet all the ceremonies of the Freemasons, and the only sentence passed on him is:

"He is a scoundrel. We knew that before!"

A prince in Naples, and M. Hamilton in his own house, perform the miracle of St. Januarius; they are, most likely, very merry over their performance, and many more with them. Yet the king wears on his royal breast a star with the following device around the image of St. Januarius: 'In sanguine foedus'. In our days everything is inconsistent, and nothing has any meaning. Yet it is right to go ahead, for to stop on the road would be to go from bad to worse.

We left Lyons in the public diligence, and were five days on our road to Paris. Baletti had given notice of his departure to his family; they therefore knew when to expect him. We were eight in the coach and our seats were very uncomfortable, for it was a large oval in shape, so that no one had a corner. If that vehicle had been built in a country where equality was a principle hallowed by the laws, it would not have been a bad illustration. I thought it was absurd, but I was in a foreign country, and I said nothing. Besides, being an Italian, would it have been right for me not to admire everything which was French, and particularly in France?—Example, an oval diligence: I respected the fashion, but I found it detestable, and the singular motion of that vehicle had the same effect upon me as the rolling of a ship in a heavy sea. Yet it was well hung, but the worst jolting would have disturbed me less.

As the diligence undulates in the rapidity of its pace, it has been called a gondola, but I was a judge of gondolas, and I thought that there was no family likeness between the coach and the Venetian boats which, with two hearty rowers, glide along so swiftly and smoothly. The effect of the movement was that I had to throw up whatever was on my stomach. My travelling companions thought me bad company, but they did not say so. I was in France and among Frenchmen, who know what politeness is. They only remarked that very likely I had eaten too much at my supper, and a Parisian abbe, in order to excuse me, observed that my stomach was weak. A discussion arose.

"Gentlemen," I said, in my vexation, and rather angrily, "you are all wrong, for my stomach is excellent, and I have not had any supper."

Thereupon an elderly man told me, with a voice full of sweetness, that I ought not to say that the gentlemen were wrong, though I might say that they were not right, thus imitating Cicero, who, instead of declaring to the Romans that Catilina and the other conspirators were dead, only said that they had lived.

"Is it not the same thing?"

"I beg your pardon, sir, one way of speaking is polite, the other is not." And after treating me to a long dissection on politeness, he concluded by saying, with a smile, "I suppose you are an Italian?"

"Yes, I am, but would you oblige me by telling me how you have found it out?"

"Oh! I guessed it from the attention with which you have listened to my long prattle."

Everybody laughed, and, I, much pleased with his eccentricity, began to coax him. He was the tutor of a young boy of twelve or thirteen years who was seated near him. I made him give me during the journey lessons in French politeness, and when we parted he took me apart in a friendly manner, saying that he wished to make me a small present.

"What is it?"

"You must abandon, and, if I may say so, forget, the particle 'non', which you use frequently at random. 'Non' is not a French word; instead of that unpleasant monosyllable, say, 'Pardon'. 'Non' is equal to giving the lie: never say it, or prepare yourself to give and to receive sword-stabs every moment."

"I thank you, monsieur, your present is very precious, and I promise you never to say non again."

During the first fortnight of my stay in Paris, it seemed to me that I had become the most faulty man alive, for I never ceased begging pardon. I even thought, one evening at the theatre, that I should have a quarrel for having begged somebody's pardon in the wrong place. A young fop, coming to the pit, trod on my foot, and I hastened to say,

"Your pardon, sir."

"Sir, pardon me yourself."

"No, yourself."

"Yourself!"

"Well, sir, let us pardon and embrace one another!" The embrace put a stop to the discussion.

One day during the journey, having fallen asleep from fatigue in the inconvenient gondola, someone pushed my arm.

"Ah, sir! look at that mansion!"

"I see it; what of it?"

"Ah! I pray you, do you not find it. . ."

"I find nothing particular; and you?"

"Nothing wonderful, if it were not situated at a distance of forty leagues from Paris. But here! Ah! would my 'badauds' of Parisians believe that such a beautiful mansion can be found forty leagues distant from the metropolis? How ignorant a man is when he has never travelled!"

"You are quite right."

That man was a Parisian and a 'badaud' to the backbone, like a Gaul in the days of Caesar.

But if the Parisians are lounging about from morning till night, enjoying everything around them, a foreigner like myself ought to have been a greater 'badaud' than they! The difference between us was that, being accustomed to see things such as they are, I was astonished at seeing them often covered with a mask which changed their nature, while their surprise often arose from their suspecting what the mask concealed.

What delighted me, on my arrival in Paris, was the magnificent road made by Louis XV, the cleanliness of the hotels, the excellent fare they give, the quickness of the service, the excellent beds, the modest appearance of the attendant, who generally is the most accomplished girl of the house, and whose decency, modest manners, and neatness, inspire the most shameless libertine with respect. Where is the Italian who is pleased with the effrontery and the insolence of the hotel-waiters in Italy? In my days, people did not know in France what it was to overcharge; it was truly the home of foreigners. True, they had the unpleasantness of often witnessing acts of odious despotism, 'lettres de cachet', etc.; it was the despotism of a king. Since that time the French have the despotism of the people. Is it less obnoxious?

We dined at Fontainebleau, a name derived from Fontaine-belle-eau; and when we were only two leagues from Paris we saw a berlin advancing towards us. As it came near the diligence, my friend Baletti called out to the postillions to stop. In the berlin was his mother, who offered me the welcome given to an expected friend. His mother was the celebrated actress Silvia, and when I had been introduced to her she said to me;

"I hope, sir, that my son's friend will accept a share of our family supper this evening."

I accepted gratefully, sat down again in the gondola, Baletti got into the berlin with his mother, and we continued our journey.

On reaching Paris, I found a servant of Silvia's waiting for me with a coach; he accompanied me to my lodging to leave my luggage, and we repaired to Baletti's house, which was only fifty yards distant from my dwelling.

Baletti presented me to his father, who was known under the name of Mario. Silvia and Mario were the stage names assumed by M. and Madame Baletti, and at that time it was the custom in France to call the Italian actors by the names they had on the stage. 'Bon jour', Monsieur Arlequin; 'bon jour', Monsieur Pantalon: such was the manner in which the French used to address the actors who personified those characters on the stage.

VI

My Apprenticeship in Paris—Portraits—
Oddities—All Sorts of Things.

To celebrate the arrival of her son, Silvia gave a splendid supper to which she had invited all her relatives, and it was a good opportunity for me to make their acquaintance. Baletti's father, who had just recovered from a long illness, was not with us, but we had his father's sister, who was older than Mario. She was known, under her theatrical name of Flaminia, in the literary world by several translations, but I had a great wish to make her acquaintance less on that account than in consequence of the story, known throughout Italy, of the stay that three literary men of great fame had made in Paris. Those three literati were the Marquis Maffei, the Abbe Conti, and Pierre Jacques Martelli, who became enemies, according to public rumour, owing to the belief entertained by each of them that he possessed the favours of the actress, and, being men of learning, they fought with the pen. Martelli composed a satire against Maffei, in which he designated him by the anagram of Femia.

I had been announced to Flaminia as a candidate for literary fame, and she thought she honoured me by addressing me at all, but she was wrong, for she displeased me greatly by her face, her manners, her style, even by the sound of her voice. Without saying it positively, she made me understand that, being herself an illustrious member of the republic of letters, she was well aware that she was speaking to an insect. She seemed as if she wanted to dictate to everybody around her, and she very likely thought that she had the right to do so at the age of sixty, particularly towards a young novice only twenty-five years old, who had not yet contributed anything to the literary treasury. In order to please her, I spoke to her of the Abbe Conti, and I had occasion to quote two lines of that profound writer. Madam corrected me with a patronizing air for my pronunciation of the word 'scevra', which means divided, saying that it ought to be pronounced 'sceura', and she added that I ought to be very glad to have learned so much on the first day of my arrival in Paris, telling me that it would be an important day in my life.

"Madam, I came here to learn and not to unlearn. You will kindly allow me to tell you that the pronunciation of that word 'scevra' with a v, and not 'sceura' with a u, because it is a contraction of 'sceverra'."

"It remains to be seen which of us is wrong."

"You, madam, according to Ariosto, who makes 'scevra' rhyme with 'persevra', and the rhyme would be false with 'sceura', which is not an Italian word."

She would have kept up the discussion, but her husband, a man eighty years of age, told her that she was wrong. She held her tongue, but from that time she told everybody that I was an impostor.

Her husband, Louis Riccoboni, better known as Lelio, was the same who had brought the Italian company to Paris in 1716, and placed it at the service of the regent: he was a man of great merit. He had been very handsome, and justly enjoyed the esteem of the public, in consequence not only of his talent but also of the purity of his life.

During supper my principal occupation was to study Silvia, who then enjoyed the greatest reputation, and I judged her to be even above it. She was then about fifty years old, her figure was elegant, her air noble, her manners graceful and easy; she was affable, witty, kind to everybody, simple and unpretending. Her face was an enigma, for it inspired everyone with the warmest sympathy, and yet if you examined it attentively there was not one beautiful feature; she could not be called handsome, but no one could have thought her ugly. Yet she was not one of those women who are neither handsome nor ugly, for she possessed a certain something which struck one at first sight and captivated the interest. Then what was she?

Beautiful, certainly, but owing to charms unknown to all those who, not being attracted towards her by an irresistible feeling which compelled them to love her, had not the courage to study her, or the constancy to obtain a thorough knowledge of her.

Silvia was the adoration of France, and her talent was the real support of all the comedies which the greatest authors wrote for her, especially of, the plays of Marivaux, for without her his comedies would never have gone to posterity. Never was an actress found who could replace her, and to find one it would be necessary that she should unite in herself all the perfections which Silvia possessed for the difficult profession of the stage: action, voice, intelligence, wit, countenance, manners, and a deep knowledge of the human heart. In Silvia every quality was from nature, and the art which gave the last touch of perfection to her qualities was never seen.

To the qualities which I have just mentioned, Silvia added another which surrounded her with a brilliant halo, and the absence of which would not have prevented her from being the shining star of the stage: she led a virtuous life. She had been anxious to have friends, but she had dismissed all lovers, refusing to avail herself of a privilege which she could easily have enjoyed, but which would have rendered her contemptible in her own estimation. The irreproachable conduct obtained for her a reputation of respectability which, at her age, would have been held as ridiculous and even insulting by any other woman belonging to the same profession, and many ladies of the highest rank honoured her with her friendship more even than with their patronage. Never did the capricious audience of a Parisian pit dare to hiss Silvia, not even in her performance of characters which the public disliked, and it was the general opinion that she was in every way above her profession.

Silvia did not think that her good conduct was a merit, for she knew that she was virtuous only because her self-love compelled her to be so, and she never exhibited any pride or assumed any superiority towards her theatrical sisters, although, satisfied to shine by their talent or their beauty, they cared little about rendering themselves conspicuous by their virtue. Silvia loved them all, and they all loved her; she always was the first to praise, openly and with good faith, the talent of her rivals; but she lost nothing by it, because, being their superior in talent and enjoying a spotless reputation, her rivals could not rise above her.

Nature deprived that charming woman of ten year of life; she became consumptive at the age of sixty, ten years after I had made her acquaintance. The climate of Paris often proves fatal to our Italian actresses. Two years before her death I saw her perform the character of Marianne in the comedy of Marivaux, and in spite of her age and declining health the illusion was complete. She died in my presence, holding her daughter in her arms, and she was giving her the advice of a tender mother five minutes before she breathed her last. She was honourably buried in the church of St. Sauveur, without the slightest opposition from the venerable priest, who, far from sharing the anti-christain intolerancy of the clergy in general, said that her profession as an actress had not hindered her from being a good Christian, and that the earth was the common mother of all human beings, as Jesus Christ had been the Saviour of all mankind.

You will forgive me, dear reader, if I have made you attend the funeral of Silvia ten years before her death; believe me I have no intention of performing a miracle; you may console yourself with the idea that I shall spare you that unpleasant task when poor Silvia dies.

Her only daughter, the object of her adoration, was seated next to her at the supper-table. She was then only nine years old, and being entirely taken up by her mother I paid no attention to her; my interest in her was to come.

After the supper, which was protracted to a late hour, I repaired to the house of Madame Quinson, my landlady, where I found myself very comfortable. When I woke in the morning, the said Madame Quinson came to my room to tell me that a servant was outside and wished to offer me his services. I asked her to send him in, and I saw a man of very small stature; that did not please me, and I told him so.

"My small stature, your honour, will be a guarantee that I shall never borrow your clothes to go to some amorous rendezvous."

"Your name?"

"Any name you please."

"What do you mean? I want the name by which you are known."

"I have none. Every master I serve calls me according to his fancy, and I have served more than fifty in my life. You may call me what you like."

"But you must have a family name."

"I never had any family. I had a name, I believe, in my young days, but I have forgotten it since I have been in service. My name has changed with every new master."

"Well! I shall call you Esprit."

"You do me a great honour."

"Here, go and get me change for a Louis."

"I have it, sir."

"I see you are rich."

"At your service, sir."

"Where can I enquire about you?"

"At the agency for servants. Madame Quinson, besides, can answer your enquiries. Everybody in Paris knows me."

"That is enough. I shall give you thirty sous a day; you must find your own clothes: you will sleep where you like, and you must be here at seven o'clock every morning."

Baletti called on me and entreated me to take my meals every day at his house. After his visit I told Esprit to take me to the Palais-Royal, and I left him at the gates. I felt the greatest curiosity about that renowned garden, and at first I examined everything. I see a rather fine garden, walks lined with big trees, fountains, high houses all round the garden, a great many men and women walking about, benches here and there forming shops for the sale of newspapers, perfumes, tooth-picks, and other trifles. I see a quantity of chairs for hire at the rate of one sou, men reading the newspaper under the shade of the trees, girls and men breakfasting either alone or in company, waiters who were rapidly going up and down a narrow staircase hidden under the foliage.

I sit down at a small table: a waiter comes immediately to enquire my wishes. I ask for some chocolate made with water; he brings me some, but very bad, although served in a splendid silver-gilt cup. I tell him to give me some coffee, if it is good.

"Excellent, I made it myself yesterday."

"Yesterday! I do not want it."

"The milk is very good."

"Milk! I never drink any. Make me a cup of fresh coffee without milk."

"Without milk! Well, sir, we never make coffee but in the afternoon. Would you like a good bavaroise, or a decanter of orgeat?"

"Yes, give me the orgeat."

I find that beverage delicious, and make up my mind to have it daily for my breakfast. I enquire from the waiter whether there is any news; he answers that the dauphine has been delivered of a prince. An abbe, seated at a table close by, says to him,—

"You are mad, she has given birth to a princess."

A third man comes forward and exclaims,—

"I have just returned from Versailles, and the dauphine has not been delivered either of a prince or of a princess."

Then, turning towards me, he says that I look like a foreigner, and when I say that I am an Italian he begins to speak to me of the court, of the city, of the theatres, and at last he offers to accompany me everywhere. I thank him and take my leave. The abbe rises at the same time, walks with me, and tells me the names of all the women we meet in the garden.

A young man comes up to him, they embrace one another, and the abbe presents him to me as a learned Italian scholar. I address him in Italian, and he answers very wittily, but his way of speaking makes me smile, and I tell him why. He expressed himself exactly in the style of Boccacio. My remark pleases him, but I soon prove to him that it is not the right way to speak, however perfect may have been the language of that ancient writer. In less than a quarter of an hour we are excellent friends, for we find that our tastes are the same.

My new friend was a poet as I was; he was an admirer of Italian literature, while I admired the French.

We exchanged addresses, and promise to see one another very often.

I see a crowd in one corner of the garden, everybody standing still and looking up. I enquire from my friend whether there is anything wonderful going on.

"These persons are watching the meridian; everyone holds his watch in his hand in order to regulate it exactly at noon."

"Is there not a meridian everywhere?"

"Yes, but the meridian of the Palais-Royal is the most exact."

I laugh heartily.

"Why do you laugh?"

"Because it is impossible for all meridians not to be the same. That is true 'badauderie'."

My friend looks at me for a moment, then he laughs likewise, and supplies me with ample food to ridicule the worthy Parisians. We leave the Palais-Royal through the main gate, and I observe another crowd of people before a shop, on the sign-board of which I read "At the Sign of the Civet Cat."

"What is the matter here?"

"Now, indeed, you are going to laugh. All these honest persons are waiting their turn to get their snuff-boxes filled."

"Is there no other dealer in snuff?"

"It is sold everywhere, but for the last three weeks nobody will use any snuff but that sold at the 'Civet Cat.'"

"Is it better than anywhere else?"

"Perhaps it is not as good, but since it has been brought into fashion by the Duchesse de Chartres, nobody will have any other."

"But how did she manage to render it so fashionable?"

"Simply by stopping her carriage two or three times before the shop to have her snuff-box filled, and by saying aloud to the young girl who handed back the box that her snuff was the very best in Paris. The 'badauds', who never fail to congregate near the carriage of princes, no matter if they have seen them a hundred times, or if they know them to be as ugly as monkeys, repeated the words of the duchess everywhere, and that was enough to send here all the snuff-takers of the capital in a hurry. This woman will make a fortune, for she sells at least one hundred crowns' worth of snuff every day."

"Very likely the duchess has no idea of the good she has done."

"Quite the reverse, for it was a cunning artifice on her part. The duchess, feeling interested in the newly-married young woman, and wishing to serve her in a delicate manner, thought of that expedient which has met with complete success. You cannot imagine how kind Parisians are. You are now in the only country in the world where wit can make a fortune by selling either a genuine or a false article: in the first case, it receives the welcome of intelligent and talented people, and in the second, fools are always ready to reward it, for silliness is truly a characteristic of the people here, and, however wonderful it may appear, silliness is the daughter of wit. Therefore it is not a paradox to say that the French would be wiser if they were less witty.

"The gods worshipped here although no altars are raised for them—are Novelty and Fashion. Let a man run, and everybody will run after him. The crowd will not stop, unless the man is proved to be mad; but to prove it is indeed a difficult task, because we have a crowd of men who, mad from their birth, are still considered wise.

"The snuff of the 'Civet Cat' is but one example of the facility with which the crowd can be attracted to one particular spot. The king was one day hunting, and found himself at the Neuilly Bridge; being thirsty, he wanted a glass of ratafia. He stopped at the door of a drinking-booth, and by the most lucky chance the poor keeper of the place happened to have a bottle of that liquor. The king, after he had drunk a small glass, fancied a second one, and said that he had never tasted such delicious ratafia in his life. That was enough to give the ratafia of the good man of Neuilly the reputation of being the best in Europe: the king had said so. The consequence was that the most brilliant society frequented the tavern of the delighted publican, who is now a very wealthy man, and has built on the very spot a splendid house on which can be read the following rather comic motto: 'Ex liquidis solidum,' which certainly came out of the head of one of the forty immortals. Which gods must the worthy tavern-keeper worship? Silliness, frivolity, and mirth."

"It seems to me," I replied, "that such approval, such ratification of the opinion expressed by the king, the princes of the blood, etc., is rather a proof of the affection felt for them by the nation, for the French carry that affection to such an extent that they believe them infallible."

"It is certain that everything here causes foreigners to believe that the French people adore the king, but all thinking men here know well enough that there is more show than reality in that adoration, and the court has no confidence in it. When the king comes to Paris, everybody calls out, 'Vive le Roi!' because some idle fellow begins, or because some policeman has given the signal from the midst of the crowd, but it is really a cry which has no importance, a cry given out of cheerfulness, sometimes out of fear, and which the king himself does not accept as gospel. He does not feel comfortable in Paris, and he prefers being in Versailles, surrounded by twenty-five thousand men who protect him against the fury of that same people of Paris, who, if ever they became wiser, might very well one day call out, 'Death to the King!' instead of, 'Long life to the King!' Louis XIV was well aware of it, and several councillors of the upper chamber lost their lives for having advised the assembling of the states-general in order to find some remedy for the misfortunes of the country. France never had any love for any kings, with the exception of St. Louis, of Louis XII, and of the great and good Henry IV; and even in the last case the love of the nation was not sufficient to defend the king against the dagger of the Jesuits, an accursed race, the enemy of nations as well as of kings. The present king, who is weak and entirely led by his ministers, said candidly at the time he was just recovering from illness, 'I am surprised at the rejoicings of the people in consequence of my health being restored, for I cannot imagine why they should love me so dearly.' Many kings might repeat the same words, at least if love is to be measured according to the amount of good actually done. That candid remark of Louis XV has been highly praised, but some philosopher of the court ought to have informed him that he was so much loved because he had been surnamed 'le bien aime'."

"Surname or nickname; but are there any philosophers at the court of France?"

"No, for philosophers and courtiers are as widely different as light and darkness; but there are some men of intelligence who champ the bit from motives of ambition and interest."

As we were thus conversing, M. Patu (such was the name of my new acquaintance) escorted me as far as the door of Silvia's house; he congratulated me upon being one of her friends, and we parted company.

I found the amiable actress in good company. She introduced me to all her guests, and gave me some particulars respecting every one of them. The name of Crebillon struck my ear.

"What, sir!" I said to him, "am I fortunate enough to see you? For eight years you have charmed me, for eight years I have longed to know you. Listen, I beg 'of you."

I then recited the finest passage of his 'Zenobie et Rhadamiste', which I had translated into blank verse. Silvia was delighted to see the pleasure enjoyed by Crebillon in hearing, at the age of eighty, his own lines in a language which he knew thoroughly and loved as much as his own. He himself recited the same passage in French, and politely pointed out the parts in which he thought that I had improved on the original. I thanked him, but I was not deceived by his compliment.

We sat down to supper, and, being asked what I had already seen in Paris, I related everything I had done, omitting only my conversation with Patu. After I had spoken for a long time, Crebillon, who had evidently observed better than anyone else the road I had chosen in order to learn the good as well as the bad qualities by his countrymen, said to me,

"For the first day, sir, I think that what you have done gives great hopes of you, and without any doubt you will make rapid progress. You tell your story well, and you speak French in such a way as to be perfectly understood; yet all you say is only Italian dressed in French. That is a novelty which causes you to be listened to with interest, and which captivates the attention of your audience; I must even add that your Franco-Italian language is just the thing to enlist in your favour the sympathy of those who listen to you, because it is singular, new, and because you are in a country where everybody worships those two divinities—novelty and singularity. Nevertheless, you must begin to-morrow and apply yourself in good earnest, in order to acquire a thorough knowledge of our language, for the same persons who warmly applaud you now, will, in two or three months, laugh at you."

"I believe it, sir, and that is what I fear; therefore the principal object of my visit here is to devote myself entirely to the study of the French language. But, sir, how shall I find a teacher? I am a very unpleasant pupil, always asking questions, curious, troublesome, insatiable, and even supposing that I could meet with the teacher I require, I am afraid I am not rich enough to pay him."

"For fifty years, sir, I have been looking out for a pupil such as you have just described yourself, and I would willingly pay you myself if you would come to my house and receive my lessons. I reside in the Marais, Rue de Douze Portes. I have the best Italian poets. I will make you translate them into French, and you need not be afraid of my finding you insatiable."

I accepted with joy. I did not know how to express my gratitude, but both his offer and the few words of my answer bore the stamp of truth and frankness.

Crebillon was a giant; he was six feet high, and three inches taller than I. He had a good appetite, could tell a good story without laughing, was celebrated for his witty repartees and his sociable manners, but he spent his life at home, seldom going out, and seeing hardly anyone because he always had a pipe in his mouth and was surrounded by at least twenty cats, with which he would amuse himself all day. He had an old housekeeper, a cook, and a man-servant. His housekeeper had the management of everything; she never allowed him to be in need of anything, and she gave no account of his money, which she kept altogether, because he never asked her to render any accounts. The expression of Crebillon's face was that of the lion's or of the cat's, which is the same thing. He was one of the royal censors, and he told me that it was an amusement for him. His housekeeper was in the habit of reading him the works brought for his examination, and she would stop reading when she came to a passage which, in her opinion, deserved his censure, but sometimes they were of a different opinion, and then their discussions were truly amusing. I once heard the housekeeper send away an author with these words:

"Come again next week; we have had no time to examine your manuscript."

During a whole year I paid M. Crebillon three visits every week, and from him I learned all I know of the French language, but I found it impossible to get rid of my Italian idioms. I remark that turn easily enough when I meet with it in other people, but it flows naturally from my pen without my being aware of it. I am satisfied that, whatever I may do, I shall never be able to recognize it any more than I can find out in what consists the bad Latin style so constantly alleged against Livy.

I composed a stanza of eight verses on some subject which I do not recollect, and I gave it to Crebillon, asking him to correct it. He read it attentively, and said to me,

"These eight verses are good and regular, the thought is fine and truly poetical, the style is perfect, and yet the stanza is bad."

"How so?"

"I do not know. I cannot tell you what is wanting. Imagine that you see a man handsome, well made, amiable, witty-in fact, perfect, according to your most severe judgment. A woman comes in, sees him, looks at him, and goes away telling you that the man does not please her. 'But what fault do you find in him, madam?' 'None, only he does not please me.' You look again at the man, you examine him a second time, and you find that, in order to give him a heavenly voice, he has been deprived of that which constitutes a man, and you are compelled to acknowledge that a spontaneous feeling has stood the woman in good stead."

It was by that comparison that Crebillon explained to me a thing almost inexplicable, for taste and feeling alone can account for a thing which is subject to no rule whatever.

We spoke a great deal of Louis XIV, whom Crebillon had known well for fifteen years, and he related several very curious anecdotes which were generally unknown. Amongst other things he assured me that the Siamese ambassadors were cheats paid by Madame de Maintenon. He told us likewise that he had never finished his tragedy of Cromwell, because the king had told him one day not to wear out his pen on a scoundrel.

Crebillon mentioned likewise his tragedy of Catilina, and he told me that, in his opinion, it was the most deficient of his works, but that he never would have consented, even to make a good tragedy, to represent Caesar as a young man, because he would in that case have made the public laugh, as they would do if Madea were to appear previous to her acquaintances with Jason.

He praised the talent of Voltaire very highly, but he accused him of having stolen from him, Crebillon, the scene of the senate. He, however, rendered him full justice, saying that he was a true historian, and able to write history as well as tragedies, but that he unfortunately adulterated history by mixing with it such a number of light anecdotes and tales for the sake of rendering it more attractive. According to Crebillon, the Man with the Iron Mask was nothing but an idle tale, and he had been assured of it by Louis XIV himself.

On the day of my first meeting with Crebillon at Silvia's, "Cenie", a play by Madame de Graffigny, was performed at the Italian Theatre, and I went away early in order to get a good seat in the pit.

The ladies all covered with diamonds, who were taking possession of the private boxes, engrossed all my interest and all my attention. I wore a very fine suit, but my open ruffles and the buttons all along my coat shewed at once that I was a foreigner, for the fashion was not the same in Paris. I was gaping in the air and listlessly looking round, when a gentleman, splendidly dressed, and three times stouter than I, came up and enquired whether I was a foreigner. I answered affirmatively, and he politely asked me how I liked Paris. I praised Paris very warmly. But at that moment a very stout lady, brilliant with diamonds, entered the box near us. Her enormous size astonished me, and, like a fool, I said to the gentleman:

"Who is that fat sow?"

"She is the wife of this fat pig."

"Ah! I beg your pardon a thousand times!"

But my stout gentleman cared nothing for my apologies, and very far from being angry he almost choked with laughter. This was the happy result of the practical and natural philosophy which Frenchmen cultivate so well, and which insures the happiness of their existence under an appearance of frivolity!

I was confused, I was in despair, but the stout gentleman continued to laugh heartily. At last he left the pit, and a minute afterwards I saw him enter the box and speak to his wife. I was keeping an eye on them without daring to look at them openly, and suddenly the lady, following the example of her husband, burst into a loud laugh. Their mirth making me more uncomfortable, I was leaving the pit, when the husband called out to me, "Sir! Sir!"

"I could not go away without being guilty of impoliteness, and I went up to their box. Then, with a serious countenance and with great affability, he begged my pardon for having laughed so much, and very graciously invited me to come to his house and sup with them that same evening. I thanked him politely, saying that I had a previous engagement. But he renewed his entreaties, and his wife pressing me in the most engaging manner I told them, in order to prove that I was not trying to elude their invitation, that I was expected to sup at Silvia's house.

"In that case I am certain," said the gentleman, "of obtaining your release if you do not object. Allow me to go myself to Silvia."

It would have been uncourteous on my part to resist any longer. He left the box and returned almost immediately with my friend Baletti, who told me that his mother was delighted to see me making such excellent acquaintances, and that she would expect to see me at dinner the next day. He whispered to me that my new acquaintance was M. de Beauchamp, Receiver-General of Taxes.

As soon as the performance was over, I offered my hand to madame, and we drove to their mansion in a magnificent carriage. There I found the abundance or rather the profusion which in Paris is exhibited by the men of finance; numerous society, high play, good cheer, and open cheerfulness. The supper was not over till one o'clock in the morning. Madame's private carriage drove me to my lodgings. That house offered me a kind welcome during the whole of my stay in Paris, and I must add that my new friends proved very useful to me. Some persons assert that foreigners find the first fortnight in Paris very dull, because a little time is necessary to get introduced, but I was fortunate enough to find myself established on as good a footing as I could desire within twenty-four hours, and the consequence was that I felt delighted with Paris, and certain that my stay would prove an agreeable one.

The next morning Patu called and made me a present of his prose panegyric on the Marechal de Saxe. We went out together and took a walk in the Tuileries, where he introduced me to Madame du Boccage, who made a good jest in speaking of the Marechal de Saxe.

"It is singular," she said, "that we cannot have a 'De profundis' for a man who makes us sing the 'Te Deum' so often."

As we left the Tuileries, Patu took me to the house of a celebrated actress of the opera, Mademoiselle Le Fel, the favourite of all Paris, and member of the Royal Academy of Music. She had three very young and charming children, who were fluttering around her like butterflies.

"I adore them," she said to me.

"They deserve adoration for their beauty," I answered, "although they have all a different cast of countenance."

"No wonder! The eldest is the son of the Duke d'Anneci, the second of Count d'Egmont, and the youngest is the offspring of Maison-Rouge, who has just married the Romainville."

"Ah! pray excuse me, I thought you were the mother of the three."

"You were not mistaken, I am their mother."

As she said these words she looked at Patu, and both burst into hearty laughter which did not make me blush, but which shewed me my blunder.

I was a novice in Paris, and I had not been accustomed to see women encroach upon the privilege which men alone generally enjoy. Yet mademoiselle Le Fel was not a bold-faced woman; she was even rather ladylike, but she was what is called above prejudices. If I had known the manners of the time better, I should have been aware that such things were every-day occurrences, and that the noblemen who thus sprinkled their progeny everywhere were in the habit of leaving their children in the hands of their mothers, who were well paid. The more fruitful, therefore, these ladies were, the greater was their income.

My want of experience often led me into serious blunders, and Mademoiselle Le Fel would, I have no doubt, have laughed at anyone telling her that I had some wit, after the stupid mistake of which I had been guilty.

Another day, being at the house of Lani, ballet-master of the opera, I saw five or six young girls of thirteen or fourteen years of age accompanied by their mothers, and all exhibiting that air of modesty which is the characteristic of a good education. I addressed a few gallant words to them, and they answered me with down-cast eyes. One of them having complained of the headache, I offered her my smelling-bottle, and one of her companions said to her,

"Very likely you did not sleep well last night."

"Oh! it is not that," answered the modest-looking Agnes, "I think I am in the family-way."

On receiving this unexpected reply from a girl I had taken for a maiden, I said to her,

"I should never have supposed that you were married, madam."

She looked at me with evident surprise for a moment, then she turned towards her friend, and both began to laugh immoderately. Ashamed, but for them more than myself, I left the house with a firm resolution never again to take virtue for granted in a class of women amongst whom it is so scarce. To look for, even to suppose, modesty, amongst the nymphs of the green room, is, indeed, to be very foolish; they pride themselves upon having none, and laugh at those who are simple enough to suppose them better than they are.

Thanks to my friend Patu, I made the acquaintance of all the women who enjoyed some reputation in Paris. He was fond of the fair sex, but unfortunately for him he had not a constitution like mine, and his love of pleasure killed him very early. If he had lived, he would have gone down to posterity in the wake of Voltaire, but he paid the debt of nature at the age of thirty.

I learned from him the secret which several young French literati employ in order to make certain of the perfection of their prose, when they want to write anything requiring as perfect a style as they can obtain, such as panegyrics, funeral orations, eulogies, dedications, etc. It was by surprise that I wrested that secret from Patu.

Being at his house one morning, I observed on his table several sheets of paper covered with dode-casyllabic blank verse.

I read a dozen of them, and I told him that, although the verses were very fine, the reading caused me more pain than pleasure.

"They express the same ideas as the panegyric of the Marechal de Saxe, but I confess that your prose pleases me a great deal more."

"My prose would not have pleased you so much, if it had not been at first composed in blank verse."

"Then you take very great trouble for nothing."

"No trouble at all, for I have not the slightest difficulty in writing that sort of poetry. I write it as easily as prose."

"Do you think that your prose is better when you compose it from your own poetry?"

"No doubt of it, it is much better, and I also secure the advantage that my prose is not full of half verses which flow from the pen of the writer without his being aware of it."

"Is that a fault?"

"A great one and not to be forgiven. Prose intermixed with occasional verses is worse than prosaic poetry."

"Is it true that the verses which, like parasites, steal into a funeral oration, must be sadly out of place?"

"Certainly. Take the example of Tacitus, who begins his history of Rome by these words: 'Urbem Roman a principio reges habuere'. They form a very poor Latin hexameter, which the great historian certainly never made on purpose, and which he never remarked when he revised his work, for there is no doubt that, if he had observed it, he would have altered that sentence. Are not such verses considered a blemish in Italian prose?"

"Decidedly. But I must say that a great many poor writers have purposely inserted such verses into their prose, believing that they would make it more euphonious. Hence the tawdriness which is justly alleged against much Italian literature. But I suppose you are the only writer who takes so much pains."

"The only one? Certainly not. All the authors who can compose blank verses very easily, as I can, employ them when they intend to make a fair copy of their prose. Ask Crebillon, the Abby de Voisenon, La Harpe, anyone you like, and they will all tell you the same thing.

Voltaire was the first to have recourse to that art in the small pieces in which his prose is truly charming. For instance, the epistle to Madame du Chatelet, which is magnificent. Read it, and if you find a single hemistich in it I will confess myself in the wrong."

I felt some curiosity about the matter, and I asked Crebillon about it. He told me that Fatu was right, but he added that he had never practised that art himself.

Patu wished very much to take me to the opera in order to witness the effect produced upon me by the performance, which must truly astonish an Italian. 'Les Fetes Venitiennes' was the title of the opera which was in vogue just then—a title full of interest for me. We went for our forty sous to the pit, in which, although the audience was standing, the company was excellent, for the opera was the favourite amusement of the Parisians.

After a symphony, very fine in its way and executed by an excellent orchestra, the curtain rises, and I see a beautiful scene representing the small St. Mark's Square in Venice, taken from the Island of St. George, but I am shocked to see the ducal palace on my left, and the tall steeple on my right, that is to say the very reverse of reality. I laugh at this ridiculous mistake, and Patu, to whom I say why I am laughing, cannot help joining me. The music, very fine although in the ancient style, at first amused me on account of its novelty, but it soon wearied me. The melopaeia fatigued me by its constant and tedious monotony, and by the shrieks given out of season. That melopaeia, of the French replaces—at least they think so—the Greek melapaeia and our recitative which they dislike, but which they would admire if they understood Italian.

The action of the opera was limited to a day in the carnival, when the Venetians are in the habit of promenading masked in St. Mark's Square. The stage was animated by gallants, procuresses, and women amusing themselves with all sorts of intrigues. The costumes were whimsical and erroneous, but the whole was amusing. I laughed very heartily, and it was truly a curious sight for a Venetian, when I saw the Doge followed by twelve Councillors appear on the stage, all dressed in the most ludicrous style, and dancing a 'pas d'ensemble'. Suddenly the whole of the pit burst into loud applause at the appearance of a tall, well-made dancer, wearing a mask and an enormous black wig, the hair of which went half-way down his back, and dressed in a robe open in front and reaching to his heels. Patu said, almost reverently, "It is the inimitable Dupres." I had heard of him before, and became attentive. I saw that fine figure coming forward with measured steps, and when the dancer had arrived in front of the stage, he raised slowly his rounded arms, stretched them gracefully backward and forward, moved his feet with precision and lightness, took a few small steps, made some battements and pirouettes, and disappeared like a butterfly. The whole had not lasted half a minute. The applause burst from every part of the house. I was astonished, and asked my friend the cause of all those bravos.

"We applaud the grace of Dupres and, the divine harmony of his movements. He is now sixty years of age, and those who saw him forty years ago say that he is always the same."

"What! Has he never danced in a different style?"

"He could not have danced in a better one, for his style is perfect, and what can you want above perfection?"

"Nothing, unless it be a relative perfection."

"But here it is absolute. Dupres always does the same thing, and everyday we fancy we see it for the first time. Such is the power of the good and beautiful, of the true and sublime, which speak to the soul. His dance is true harmony, the real dance, of which you have no idea in Italy."

At the end of the second act, Dupres appeared again, still with a mask, and danced to a different tune, but in my opinion doing exactly the same as before. He advanced to the very footlights, and stopped one instant in a graceful attitude. Patu wanted to force my admiration, and I gave way. Suddenly everyone round me exclaimed,—

"Look! look! he is developing himself!"

And in reality he was like an elastic body which, in developing itself, would get larger. I made Patu very happy by telling him that Dupres was truly very graceful in all his movements. Immediately after him we had a female dancer, who jumped about like a fury, cutting to right and left, but heavily, yet she was applauded 'con furore'.

"This is," said Patu, "the famous Camargo. I congratulate you, my friend, upon having arrived in Paris in time to see her, for she has accomplished her twelfth lustre."

I confessed that she was a wonderful dancer.

"She is the first artist," continued my friend, "who has dared to spring and jump on a French stage. None ventured upon doing it before her, and, what is more extraordinary, she does not wear any drawers."

"I beg your pardon, but I saw. . ."

"What? Nothing but her skin which, to speak the truth, is not made of lilies and roses."

"The Camargo," I said, with an air of repentance, "does not please me. I like Dupres much better."

An elderly admirer of Camargo, seated on my left, told me that in her youth she could perform the 'saut de basque' and even the 'gargouillade', and that nobody had ever seen her thighs, although she always danced without drawers.

"But if you never saw her thighs, how do you know that she does not wear silk tights?"

"Oh! that is one of those things which can easily be ascertained. I see you are a foreigner, sir."

"You are right."

But I was delighted at the French opera, with the rapidity of the scenic changes which are done like lightning, at the signal of a whistle—a thing entirely unknown in Italy. I likewise admired the start given to the orchestra by the baton of the leader, but he disgusted me with the movements of his sceptre right and left, as if he thought that he could give life to all the instruments by the mere motion of his arm. I admired also the silence of the audience, a thing truly wonderful to an Italian, for it is with great reason that people complain of the noise made in Italy while the artists are singing, and ridicule the silence which prevails through the house as soon as the dancers make their appearance on the stage. One would imagine that all the intelligence of the Italians is in their eyes. At the same time I must observe that there is not one country in the world in which extravagance and whimsicalness cannot be found, because the foreigner can make comparisons with what he has seen elsewhere, whilst the natives are not conscious of their errors. Altogether the opera pleased me, but the French comedy captivated me. There the French are truly in their element; they perform splendidly, in a masterly manner, and other nations cannot refuse them the palm which good taste and justice must award to their superiority. I was in the habit of going there every day, and although sometimes the audience was not composed of two hundred persons, the actors were perfect. I have seen 'Le Misanthrope', 'L'Avare', 'Tartufe', 'Le Joueur', 'Le Glorieux', and many other comedies; and, no matter how often I saw them. I always fancied it was the first time. I arrived in Paris to admire Sarrazin, La Dangeville, La Dumesnil, La Gaussin, La Clairon, Preville, and several actresses who, having retired from the stage, were living upon their pension, and delighting their circle of friends. I made, amongst others, the acquaintance of the celebrated Le Vasseur. I visited them all with pleasure, and they related to me several very curious anecdotes. They were generally most kindly disposed in every way.

One evening, being in the box of Le Vasseur, the performance was composed of a tragedy in which a very handsome actress had the part of a dumb priestess.

"How pretty she is!" I said.

"Yes, charming," answered Le Vasseur, "She is the daughter of the actor who plays the confidant. She is very pleasant in company, and is an actress of good promise."

"I should be very happy to make her acquaintance."

"Oh! well; that is not difficult. Her father and mother are very worthy people, and they will be delighted if you ask them to invite you to supper. They will not disturb you; they will go to bed early, and will let you talk with their daughter as long as you please. You are in France, sir; here we know the value of life, and try to make the best of it. We love pleasure, and esteem ourselves fortunate when we can find the opportunity of enjoying life."

"That is truly charming, madam; but how could I be so bold as to invite myself to supper with worthy persons whom I do not know, and who have not the slightest knowledge of me?"

"Oh, dear me! What are you saying? We know everybody. You see how I treat you myself. After the performance, I shall be happy to introduce you, and the acquaintance will be made at once."

"I certainly must ask you to do me that honour, but another time."

"Whenever you like."

VII

My Blunders in the French Language, My Success, My Numerous Acquaintances—Louis XV—My Brother Arrives in Paris.

All the Italian actors in Paris insisted upon entertaining me, in order to shew me their magnificence, and they all did it in a sumptuous style. Carlin Bertinazzi who played Harlequin, and was a great favourite of the Parisians, reminded me that he had already seen me thirteen years before in Padua, at the time of his return from St. Petersburg with my mother. He offered me an excellent dinner at the house of Madame de la Caillerie, where he lodged. That lady was in love with him. I complimented her upon four charming children whom I saw in the house. Her husband, who was present, said to me;

"They are M. Carlin's children."

"That may be, sir, but you take care of them, and as they go by your name, of course they will acknowledge you as their father."

"Yes, I should be so legally; but M. Carlin is too honest a man not to assume the care of his children whenever I may wish to get rid of them. He is well aware that they belong to him, and my wife would be the first to complain if he ever denied it."

The man was not what is called a good, easy fellow, far from it; but he took the matter in a philosophical way, and spoke of it with calm, and even with a sort of dignity. He was attached to Carlin by a warm friendship, and such things were then very common in Paris amongst people of a certain class. Two noblemen, Boufflers and Luxembourg, had made a friendly exchange of each other's wives, and each had children by the other's wife. The young Boufflers were called Luxembourg, and the young Luxembourg were called Boufflers. The descendants of those tiercelets are even now known in France under those names. Well, those who were in the secret of that domestic comedy laughed, as a matter of course, and it did not prevent the earth from moving according to the laws of gravitation.

The most wealthy of the Italian comedians in Paris was Pantaloon, the father of Coraline and Camille, and a well-known usurer. He also invited me to dine with his family, and I was delighted with his two daughters. The eldest, Coraline, was kept by the Prince of

Monaco, son of the Duke of Valentinois, who was still alive; and Camille was enamoured of the Count of Melfort, the favourite of the Duchess of Chartres, who had just become Duchess of Orleans by the death of her father-in-law.

Coraline was not so sprightly as Camille, but she was prettier. I began to make love to her as a young man of no consequence, and at hours which I thought would not attract attention: but all hours belong by right to the established lover, and I therefore found myself sometimes with her when the Prince of Monaco called to see her. At first I would bow to the prince and withdraw, but afterwards I was asked to remain, for as a general thing princes find a tete-a-tete with their mistresses rather wearisome. Therefore we used to sup together, and they both listened, while it was my province to eat, and to relate stories.

I bethought myself of paying my court to the prince, and he received my advances very well. One morning, as I called on Coraline, he said to me,

"Ah! I am very glad to see you, for I have promised the Duchess of Rufe to present you to her, and we can go to her immediately."

Again a duchess! My star is decidedly in the ascendant. Well, let us go! We got into a 'diable', a sort of vehicle then very fashionable, and at eleven o'clock in the morning we were introduced to the duchess.

Dear reader, if I were to paint it with a faithful pen, my portrait of that lustful vixen would frighten you. Imagine sixty winters heaped upon a face plastered with rouge, a blotched and pimpled complexion, emaciated and gaunt features, all the ugliness of libertinism stamped upon the countenance of that creature relining upon the sofa. As soon as she sees me, she exclaims with rapid joy,

"Ah! this is a good-looking man! Prince, it is very amiable on your part to bring him to me. Come and sit near me, my fine fellow!"

I obeyed respectfully, but a noxious smell of musk, which seemed to me almost corpse-like, nearly upset me. The infamous duchess had raised herself on the sofa and exposed all the nakedness of the most disgusting bosom, which would have caused the most courageous man to draw back. The prince, pretending to have some engagement, left us, saying that he would send his carriage for me in a short time.

As soon as we were alone, the plastered skeleton thrust its arms forward, and, without giving me time to know what I was about, the creature gave me a horrible kiss, and then one of her hands began to stray with the most bare-faced indecency.

"Let me see, my fine cock," she said, "if you have a fine. . ."

I was shuddering, and resisted the attempt.

"Well, well! What a baby you are!" said the disgusting Messaline; "are you such a novice?"

"No, madam; but..."

"But what?"

"I have..."

"Oh, the villain!" she exclaimed, loosing her hold; "what was I going to expose myself to!"

I availed myself of the opportunity, snatched my hat, and took to my heels, afraid lest the door-keeper should stop me.

I took a coach and drove to Coraline's, where I related the adventure. She laughed heartily, and agreed with me that the prince had played me a nasty trick. She praised the presence of mind with which I had invented an impediment, but she did not give me an opportunity of proving to her that I had deceived the duchess.

Yet I was not without hope, and suspected that she did not think me sufficiently enamoured of her.

Three or four days afterwards, however, as we had supper together and alone, I told her so many things, and I asked her so clearly to make me happy or else to dismiss me, that she gave me an appointment for the next day.

"To-morrow," she said, "the prince goes to Versailles, and he will not return until the day after; we will go together to the warren to hunt ferrets, and have no doubt we shall come back to Paris pleased with one another."

"That is right."

The next day at ten o'clock we took a coach, but as we were nearing the gate of the city a vis-a-vis, with servants in a foreign livery came tip to us, and the person who was in it called out, "Stop! Stop!"

The person was the Chevalier de Wurtemburg, who, without deigning to cast even one glance on me, began to say sweet words to Coraline, and thrusting his head entirely out of his carriage he whispered to her. She answered him likewise in a whisper; then taking my hand, she said to me, laughingly,

"I have some important business with this prince; go to the warren alone, my dear friend, enjoy the hunt, and come to me to-morrow."

And saying those words she got out, took her seat in the vis-a-vis, and I found myself very much in the position of Lot's wife, but not motionless.

Dear reader, if you have ever been in such a predicament you will easily realize the rage with which I was possessed: if you have never been served in that way, so much the better for you, but it is useless for me to try to give you an idea of my anger; you would not understand me.

I was disgusted with the coach, and I jumped out of it, telling the driver to go to the devil. I took the first hack which happened to pass, and drove straight to Patu's house, to whom I related my adventure, almost foaming with rage. But very far from pitying me or sharing my anger, Patu, much wiser, laughed and said,

"I wish with all my heart that the same thing might happen to me; for you are certain of possessing our beautiful Coraline the very first time you are with her."

"I would not have her, for now I despise her heartily."

"Your contempt ought to have come sooner. But, now that is too late to discuss the matter, I offer you, as a compensation, a dinner at the Hotel du Roule."

"Most decidedly yes; it is an excellent idea. Let us go."

The Hotel du Roule was famous in Paris, and I had not been there yet. The woman who kept it had furnished the place with great elegance, and she always had twelve or fourteen well-chosen nymphs, with all the conveniences that could be desired. Good cooking, good beds, cleanliness, solitary and beautiful groves. Her cook was an artist, and her wine-cellar excellent. Her name was Madame Paris; probably an assumed name, but it was good enough for the purpose. Protected by the police, she was far enough from Paris to be certain that those who visited her liberally appointed establishment were above the middle class. Everything was strictly regulated in her house and every pleasure was taxed at a reasonable tariff. The prices were six francs for a breakfast with a nymph, twelve for dinner, and twice that sum to spend a whole night. I found the house even better than its reputation, and by far superior to the warren.

We took a coach, and Patu said to the driver,

"To Chaillot."

"I understand, your honour."

After a drive of half an hour, we stopped before a gate on which could be read, "Hotel du Roule."

The gate was closed. A porter, sporting long mustachioes, came out through a side-door and gravely examined us. He was most likely pleased with our appearance, for the gate was opened and we went in.

A woman, blind of one eye, about forty years old, but with a remnant of beauty, came up, saluted us politely, and enquired whether we wished to have dinner. Our answer being affirmative, she took us to a fine room in which we found fourteen young women, all very handsome, and dressed alike in muslin. As we entered the room, they rose and made us a graceful reverence; they were all about the same age, some with light hair, some with dark; every taste could be satisfied. We passed them in review, addressing a few words to each, and made our choice. The two we chose screamed for joy, kissed us with a voluptuousness which a novice might have mistaken for love, and took us to the garden until dinner would be ready. That garden was very large and artistically arranged to minister to the pleasures of love. Madame Paris said to us,

"Go, gentlemen, enjoy the fresh air with perfect security in every way; my house is the temple of peace and of good health."

The girl I had chosen was something like Coraline, and that made me find her delightful. But in the midst of our amorous occupations we were called to dinner. We were well served, and the dinner had given us new strength, when our single-eyed hostess came, watch in hand, to announce that time was up. Pleasure at the "Hotel du Roule" was measured by the hour.

I whispered to Patu, and, after a few philosophical considerations, addressing himself to madame la gouvernante, he said to her,

"We will have a double dose, and of course pay double."

"You are quite welcome, gentlemen."

We went upstairs, and after we had made our choice a second time, we renewed our promenade in the garden. But once more we were disagreeably surprised by the strict punctuality of the lady of the house. "Indeed! this is too much of a good thing, madam."

"Let us go up for the third time, make a third choice, and pass the whole night here."

"A delightful idea which I accept with all my heart."

"Does Madame Paris approve our plan?"

"I could not have devised a better one, gentlemen; it is a masterpiece."

When we were in the room, and after we had made a new choice, the girls laughed at the first ones who had not contrived to captivate us, and by way of revenge these girls told their companions that we were lanky fellows.

This time I was indeed astonished at my own choice. I had taken a true Aspasia, and I thanked my stars that I had passed her by the first two times, as I had now the certainty of possessing her for fourteen hours. That beauty's name was Saint Hilaire; and under that name she became famous in England, where she followed a rich lord the year after. At first, vexed because I had not remarked her before, she was proud and disdainful; but I soon proved to her that it was fortunate that my first or second choice had not fallen on her, as she would now remain longer with me. She then began to laugh, and shewed herself very agreeable.

That girl had wit, education and talent-everything, in fact, that is needful to succeed in the profession she had adopted. During the supper Patu told me in Italian that he was on the point of taking her at the very moment I chose her, and the next morning he informed me that he had slept quietly all night. The Saint Hilaire was highly pleased with me, and she boasted of it before her companions. She was the cause of my paying several visits to the Hotel du Roule, and all for her; she was very proud of my constancy.

Those visits very naturally cooled my ardour for Coraline. A singer from Venice, called Guadani, handsome, a thorough musician, and very witty, contrived to captivate her affections three weeks after my quarrel with her. The handsome fellow, who was a man only in appearance, inflamed her with curiosity if not with love, and caused a rupture with the prince, who caught her in the very act. But Coraline managed to coax him back, and, a short time after, a reconciliation took place between them, and such a good one, that a babe was the consequence of it; a girl, whom the prince named Adelaide, and to whom he gave a dowry. After the death of his father, the Duke of Valentinois, the prince left her altogether and married Mlle. de Brignole, from Genoa. Coraline became the mistress of Count de la Marche, now Prince de Conti. Coraline is now dead, as well as a son whom she had by the count, and whom his father named Count de Monreal.

Madame la Dauphine was delivered of a princess, who received the title of Madame de France.

In the month of August the Royal Academy had an exhibition at the Louvre, and as there was not a single battle piece I conceived the idea of summoning my brother to Paris. He was then in Venice, and he had great talent in that particular style. Passorelli, the only painter of battles known in France, was dead, and I thought that Francois might succeed and make a fortune. I therefore wrote to M. Grimani and to my brother; I persuaded them both, but Francois did not come to Paris till the beginning of the following year.

Louis XV, who was passionately fond of hunting, was in the habit of spending six weeks every year at the Chateau of Fontainebleau. He always returned to Versailles towards the middle of November. That trip cost him, or rather cost France, five millions of francs. He always took with him all that could contribute to the amusement of the foreign ambassadors and of his numerous court. He was followed by the French and the Italian comedians, and by the actors and actresses of the opera.

During those six weeks Fontainebleau was more brilliant than Versailles; nevertheless, the artists attached to the theatres were so numerous that the Opera, the French and Italian Comedies, remained open in Paris.

Baletti's father, who had recovered his health, was to go to Fontainebleau with Silvia and all his family. They invited me to accompany them, and to accept a lodging in a house hired by them.

It was a splendid opportunity; they were my friends, and I accepted, for I could not have met with a better occasion to see the court and all the foreign ministers. I presented myself to M. de Morosini, now Procurator at St. Mark's, and then ambassador from the Republic to the French court.

The first night of the opera he gave me permission to accompany him; the music was by Lulli. I had a seat in the pit precisely under the private box of Madame de Pompadour, whom I did not know. During the first scene the celebrated Le Maur gave a scream so shrill and so unexpected that I thought she had gone mad. I burst into a genuine laugh, not supposing that any one could possibly find fault with it. But a knight of the Order of the Holy Ghost, who was near the Marquise de Pompadour, dryly asked me what country I came from. I answered, in the same tone,

"From Venice."

"I have been there, and have laughed heartily at the recitative in your operas."

"I believe you, sir, and I feel certain that no one ever thought of objecting to your laughing."

My answer, rather a sharp one, made Madame de Pompadour laugh, and she asked me whether I truly came from down there.

"What do you mean by down there?"

"I mean Venice."

"Venice, madam, is not down there, but up there."

That answer was found more singular than the first, and everybody in the box held a consultation in order to ascertain whether Venice was down or up. Most likely they thought I was right, for I was left alone. Nevertheless, I listened to the opera without laughing; but as I had a very bad cold I blew my nose often. The same gentleman addressing himself again to me, remarked that very likely the windows of my room did not close well. That gentleman, who was unknown to me was the Marechal de Richelieu. I told him he was mistaken, for my windows were well 'calfoutrees'. Everyone in the box burst into a loud laugh, and I felt mortified, for I knew my mistake; I ought to have said 'calfeutrees'. But these 'eus' and 'ous' cause dire misery to all foreigners.

Half an hour afterwards M. de Richelieu asked me which of the two actresses pleased me most by her beauty.

"That one, sir."

"But she has ugly legs."

"They are not seen, sir; besides, whenever I examine the beauty of a woman, 'la premiere chose que j'ecarte, ce sont les jambes'."

That word said quite by chance, and the double meaning of which I did not understand, made at once an important personage of me, and everybody in the box of Madame de Pompadour was curious to know me. The marshal learned who I was from M. de Morosini, who told me that the duke would be happy to receive me. My 'jeu de mots' became celebrated, and the marshal honoured me with a very gracious welcome. Among the foreign ministers, the one to whom I attached myself most was Lord Keith, Marshal of Scotland and ambassador of the King of Prussia. I shall have occasion to speak of him.

The day after my arrival in Fontainebleau I went alone to the court, and I saw Louis XV, the handsome king, go to the chapel with the royal family and all the ladies of the court, who surprised me by their ugliness as much as the ladies of the court of Turin had astonished me by their beauty. Yet in the midst of so many ugly ones I found out a regular beauty. I enquired who she was.

"She is," answered one of my neighbours, "Madame de Brionne, more remarkable by her virtue even than by her beauty. Not only is there no scandalous story told about her, but she has never given any opportunity to scandal-mongers of inventing any adventure of which she was the heroine."

"Perhaps her adventures are not known."

"Ah, monsieur! at the court everything is known."

I went about alone, sauntering through the apartments, when suddenly I met a dozen ugly ladies who seemed to be running rather than walking; they were standing so badly upon their legs that they appeared as if they would fall forward on their faces. Some gentleman happened to be near me, curiosity impelled me to enquire where they were coming from, and where they were going in such haste.

"They are coming from the apartment of the queen who is going to dine, and the reason why they walk so badly is that their shoes have heels six inches high, which compel them to walk on their toes and with bent knees in order to avoid falling on their faces."

"But why do they not wear lower heels?"

"It is the fashion."

"What a stupid fashion!"

I took a gallery at random, and saw the king passing along, leaning with one arm on the shoulder of M. d'Argenson. "Oh, base servility!" I thought to myself. "How can a man make up his mind thus to bear the yoke, and how can a man believe himself so much above all others as to take such unwarrantable liberties!"

Louis XV had the most magnificent head it was possible to see, and he carried it with as much grace as majesty. Never did even the most skilful painter succeed in rendering justice to the expression of that beautiful head, when the king turned it on one side to look with kindness at anyone. His beauty and grace compelled love at once. As I saw him, I thought I had found the ideal majesty which I had been so surprised not to find in the king of Sardinia, and I could not entertain a doubt of Madame de Pompadour having been in love with the king when she sued for his royal attention. I was greatly mistaken, perhaps, but such a thought was natural in looking at the countenance of Louis XV.

I reached a splendid room in which I saw several courtiers walking about, and a table large enough for twelve persons, but laid out only for one.

"For whom is this table?"

"For the queen. Her majesty is now coming in."

It was the queen of France, without rouge, and very simply dressed; her head was covered with a large cap; she looked old and devout. When she was near the table, she graciously thanked two nuns who were placing a plate with fresh butter on it. She sat down, and immediately the courtiers formed a semicircle within five yards of the table; I remained near them, imitating their respectful silence.

Her majesty began to eat without looking at anyone, keeping her eyes on her plate. One of the dishes being to her taste, she desired to be helped to it a second time, and she then cast her eyes round the circle of courtiers, probably in order to see if among them there was anyone to whom she owed an account of her daintiness. She found that person, I suppose, for she said,

"Monsieur de Lowendal!"

At that name, a fine-looking man came forward with respectful inclination, and said,

"Your majesty?"

"I believe this is a fricassee of chickens."

"I am of the same opinion, madam."

After this answer, given in the most serious tone, the queen continued eating, and the marshal retreated backward to his original place. The queen finished her dinner without uttering a single word, and retired to her apartments the same way as she had come. I thought that if such was the way the queen of France took all her meals, I would not sue for the honour of being her guest.

I was delighted to have seen the famous captain who had conquered Bergen-op-Zoom, but I regretted that such a man should be compelled to give an answer about a fricassee of chickens in the serious tone of a judge pronouncing a sentence of death.

I made good use of this anecdote at the excellent dinner Silvia gave to the elite of polite and agreeable society.

A few days afterwards, as I was forming a line with a crowd of courtiers to enjoy the ever new pleasure of seeing the king go to mass, a pleasure to which must be added the advantage of looking at the naked and entirely exposed arms and bosoms of Mesdames de France, his daughters, I suddenly perceived the Cavamacchia, whom I had left in Cesena under the name of Madame Querini. If I was astonished to see her, she was as much so in meeting me in such a place. The Marquis of Saint Simon, premier 'gentilhomme' of the Prince de Conde, escorted her.

"Madame Querini in Fontainebleau?"

"You here? It reminds me of Queen Elizabeth saying,

"'Pauper ubique facet.'"

"An excellent comparison, madam."

"I am only joking, my dear friend; I am here to see the king, who does not know me; but to-morrow the ambassador will present me to his majesty."

She placed herself in the line within a yard or two from me, beside the door by which the king was to come. His majesty entered the gallery with M. de Richelieu, and looked at the so-called Madame Querini. But she very likely did not take his fancy, for, continuing to walk on, he addressed to the marshal these remarkable words, which Juliette must have overheard,

"We have handsomer women here."

In the afternoon I called upon the Venetian ambassador. I found him in numerous company, with Madame Querini sitting on his right. She addressed me in the most flattering and friendly manner; it was extraordinary conduct on the part of a giddy woman who had no cause to like me, for she was aware that I knew her thoroughly, and that I had mastered her vanity; but as I understood her manoeuvring I made up my mind not to disoblige her, and even to render her all the good offices I could; it was a noble revenge.

As she was speaking of M. Querini, the ambassador congratulated her upon her marriage with him, saying that he was glad M. Querini had rendered justice to her merit, and adding,

"I was not aware of your marriage."

"Yet it took place more than two years since," said Juliette.

"I know it for a fact," I said, in my turn; "for, two years ago, the lady was introduced as Madame Querini and with the title of excellency by General Spada to all the nobility in Cesena, where I was at that time."

"I have no doubt of it," answered the ambassador, fixing his eyes upon me, "for Querini has himself written to me on the subject."

A few minutes afterwards, as I was preparing to take my leave, the ambassador, under pretense of some letters the contents of which he wished to communicate to me, invited me to come into his private room, and he asked me what people generally thought of the marriage in Venice.

"Nobody knows it, and it is even rumoured that the heir of the house of Querini is on the point of marrying a daughter of the Grimani family; but I shall certainly send the news to Venice."

"What news?"

"That Juliette is truly Madame Querini, since your excellency will present her as such to Louis XV."

"Who told you so?"

"She did."

"Perhaps she has altered her mind."

I repeated to the ambassador the words which the king had said to M. de Richelieu after looking at Juliette.

"Then I can guess," remarked the ambassador, "why Juliette does not wish to be presented to the king."

I was informed some time afterwards that M. de Saint Quentin, the king's confidential minister, had called after mass on the handsome Venetian, and had told her that the king of France had most certainly very bad taste, because he had not thought her beauty superior to that of several ladies of his court. Juliette left Fontainebleau the next morning.

In the first part of my Memoirs I have spoken of Juliette's beauty; she had a wonderful charm in her countenance, but she had already used her advantages too long, and her beauty was beginning to fade when she arrived in Fontainebleau.

I met her again in Paris at the ambassador's, and she told me with a laugh that she had only been in jest when she called herself Madame Querini, and that I should oblige her if for the future I would call her by her real name of Countess Preati. She invited me to visit her at the Hotel de Luxembourg, where she was staying. I often called on her, for her intrigues amused me, but I was wise enough not to meddle with them.

She remained in Paris four months, and contrived to infatuate M. Ranchi, secretary of the Venetian Embassy, an amiable and learned man. He was so deeply in love that he had made up his mind to marry her; but through a caprice which she, perhaps, regretted afterwards, she ill-treated him, and the fool died of grief. Count de Canes, ambassador of Maria Theresa, had some inclination for her, as well as the Count of Zinzendorf. The person who arranged these transient and short-lived intrigues was a certain Guasco, an abbe not over-favoured with the gifts of Plutus. He was particularly ugly, and had to purchase small favours with great services.

But the man whom she really wished to marry was Count Saint Simon. He would have married her if she had not given him false addresses to make enquiries respecting her birth. The Preati family of Verona denied all knowledge of her, as a matter of course, and M. de Saint Simon, who, in spite of all his love, had not entirely lost his senses, had the courage to abandon her. Altogether, Paris did not prove an 'el dorado' for my handsome countrywoman, for she was obliged to pledge her diamonds, and to leave them behind her. After her return to Venice she married the son of the Uccelli, who sixteen years before had taken her out of her poverty. She died ten years ago.

I was still taking my French lessons with my good old Crebillon; yet my style, which was full of Italianisms, often expressed the very reverse of what I meant to say. But generally my 'quid pro quos' only resulted in curious jokes which made my fortune; and the best of it is that my gibberish did me no harm on the score of wit: on the contrary, it procured me fine acquaintances.

Several ladies of the best society begged me to teach them Italian, saying that it would afford them the opportunity of teaching me French; in such an exchange I always won more than they did.

Madame Preodot, who was one of my pupils, received me one morning; she was still in bed, and told me that she did not feel disposed to have a lesson, because she had taken medicine the night previous. Foolishly translating an Italian idiom, I asked her, with an air of deep interest, whether she had well 'decharge'?

"Sir, what a question! You are unbearable."

I repeated my question; she broke out angrily again.

"Never utter that dreadful word."

"You are wrong in getting angry; it is the proper word."

"A very dirty word, sir, but enough about it. Will you have some breakfast?"

"No, I thank you. I have taken a 'cafe' and two 'Savoyards'."

"Dear me! What a ferocious breakfast! Pray, explain yourself."

"I say that I have drunk a cafe and eaten two Savoyards soaked in it, and that is what I do every morning."

"You are stupid, my good friend. A cafe is the establishment in which coffee is sold, and you ought to say that you have drunk 'use tasse de cafe'"

"Good indeed! Do you drink the cup? In Italy we say a 'caffs', and we are not foolish enough to suppose that it means the coffee-house."

"He will have the best of it! And the two 'Savoyards', how did you swallow them?"

"Soaked in my coffee, for they were not larger than these on your table."

"And you call these 'Savoyards'? Say biscuits."

"In Italy, we call them 'Savoyards' because they were first invented in Savoy; and it is not my fault if you imagined that I had swallowed two of the porters to be found at the corner of the streets—big fellows whom you call in Paris Savoyards, although very often they have never been in Savoy."

Her husband came in at that moment, and she lost no time in relating the whole of our conversation. He laughed heartily, but he said I was right. Her niece arrived a few minutes after; she was a young girl about fourteen years of age, reserved, modest, and very intelligent. I had given her five or six lessons in Italian, and as she was very fond of that language and studied diligently she was beginning to speak.

Wishing to pay me her compliments in Italian, she said to me,

"'Signore, sono in cantata di vi Vader in bona salute'."

"I thank you, mademoiselle; but to translate 'I am enchanted', you must say 'ho pacer', and for to see you, you must say 'di vedervi'."

"I thought, sir, that the 'vi' was to be placed before."

"No, mademoiselle, we always put it behind."

Monsieur and Madame Preodot were dying with laughter; the young lady was confused, and I in despair at having uttered such a gross absurdity; but it could not be helped. I took a book sulkily, in the hope of putting a stop to their mirth, but it was of no use: it lasted a week. That uncouth blunder soon got known throughout Paris, and gave me a sort of reputation which I lost little by little, but only when I understood the double meanings of words better. Crebillon was much amused with my blunder, and he told me that I ought to have said after instead of behind. Ah! why have not all languages the same genius! But if the French laughed at my mistakes in speaking their language, I took my revenge amply by turning some of their idioms into ridicule.

"Sir," I once said to a gentleman, "how is your wife?"

"You do her great honour, sir."

"Pray tell me, sir, what her honour has to do with her health?"

I meet in the Bois de Boulogne a young man riding a horse which he cannot master, and at last he is thrown. I stop the horse, run to the assistance of the young man and help him up.

"Did you hurt yourself, sir?"

"Oh, many thanks, sir, au contraire."

"Why au contraire! The deuce! It has done you good? Then begin again, sir."

And a thousand similar expressions entirely the reverse of good sense. But it is the genius of the language.

I was one day paying my first visit to the wife of President de N—, when her nephew, a brilliant butterfly, came in, and she introduced me to him, mentioning my name and my country.

"Indeed, sir, you are Italian?" said the young man. "Upon my word, you present yourself so gracefully that I would have betted you were French."

"Sir, when I saw you, I was near making the same mistake; I would have betted you were Italian."

Another time, I was dining at Lady Lambert's in numerous and brilliant company. Someone remarked on my finger a cornelian ring on which was engraved very beautifully the head of Louis XV. My ring went round the table, and everybody thought that the likeness was striking.

A young marquise, who had the reputation of being a great wit, said to me in the most serious tone,

"It is truly an antique?"

"The stone, madam, undoubtedly."

Everyone laughed except the thoughtless young beauty, who did not take any notice of it. Towards the end of the dinner, someone spoke of the rhinoceros, which was then shewn for twenty-four sous at the St. Germain's Fair.

"Let us go and see it!" was the cry.

We got into the carriages, and reached the fair. We took several turns before we could find the place. I was the only gentleman; I was taking care of two ladies in the midst of the crowd, and the witty marquise was walking in front of us. At the end of the alley where we had been told that we would find the animal, there was a man placed to receive the money of the visitors. It is true that the man, dressed in the African fashion, was very dark and enormously stout, yet he had a human and very masculine form, and the beautiful marquise had no business to make a mistake. Nevertheless, the thoughtless young creature went up straight to him and said,

"Are you the rhinoceros, sir?"

"Go in, madam, go in."

We were dying with laughing; and the marquise, when she had seen the animal, thought herself bound to apologize to the master; assuring him that she had never seen a rhinoceros in her life, and therefore he could not feel offended if she had made a mistake.

One evening I was in the foyer of the Italian Comedy, where between the acts the highest noblemen were in the habit of coming, in order to converse and joke with the actresses who used to sit there waiting for their turn to appear on the stage, and I was seated near Camille, Coraline's sister, whom I amused by making love to her. A young councillor, who objected to my occupying Camille's attention, being a very conceited fellow, attacked me upon some remark I made respecting an Italian play, and took the liberty of shewing his bad temper by criticizing my native country. I was answering him in an indirect way, looking all the time at Camille, who was laughing. Everybody had congregated around us and was attentive to the discussion, which, being carried on as an assault of wit, had nothing to make it unpleasant.

But it seemed to take a serious turn when the young fop, turning the conversation on the police of the city, said that for some time it had been dangerous to walk alone at night through the streets of Paris.

"During the last month," he added, "the Place de Greve has seen the hanging of seven men, among whom there were five Italians. An extraordinary circumstance."

"Nothing extraordinary in that," I answered; "honest men generally contrive to be hung far away from their native country; and as a proof of it, sixty Frenchmen have been hung in the course of last year between Naples, Rome, and Venice. Five times twelve are sixty; so you see that it is only a fair exchange."

The laughter was all on my side, and the fine councillor went away rather crestfallen. One of the gentlemen present at the discussion, finding my answer to his taste, came up to Camille, and asked her in a whisper who I was. We got acquainted at once.

It was M. de Marigni, whom I was delighted to know for the sake of my brother whose arrival in Paris I was expecting every day. M. de Marigni was superintendent of the royal buildings, and the Academy of Painting was under his jurisdiction. I mentioned my brother to him, and he graciously promised to protect him. Another young nobleman, who conversed with me, invited me to visit him. It was the Duke de Matalona.

I told him that I had seen him, then only a child, eight years before in Naples, and that I was under great obligations to his uncle, Don Lelio. The young duke was delighted, and we became intimate friends.

My brother arrived in Paris in the spring of 1751, and he lodged with me at Madame Quinson's. He began at once to work with success for private individuals; but his main idea being to compose a picture to be submitted to the judgment of the Academy, I introduced him to M.

de Marigni, who received him with great distinction, and encouraged him by assuring him of his protection. He immediately set to work with great diligence.

M. de Morosini had been recalled, and M. de Mocenigo had succeeded him as ambassador of the Republic. M. de Bragadin had recommended me to him, and he tendered a friendly welcome both to me and to my brother, in whose favour he felt interested as a Venetian, and as a young artist seeking to build up a position by his talent.

M. de Mocenigo was of a very pleasant nature; he liked gambling although he was always unlucky at cards; he loved women, and he was not more fortunate with them because he did not know how to manage them. Two years after his arrival in Paris he fell in love with Madame de Colande, and, finding it impossible to win her affections, he killed himself.

Madame la Dauphine was delivered of a prince, the Duke of Burgundy, and the rejoicings indulged in at the birth of that child seem to me incredible now, when I see what the same nation is doing against the king. The people want to be free; it is a noble ambition, for mankind are not made to be the slaves of one man; but with a nation populous, great, witty, and giddy, what will be the end of that revolution? Time alone can tell us.

The Duke de Matalona procured me the acquaintance of the two princes, Don Marc Antoine and Don Jean Baptiste Borghese, from Rome, who were enjoying themselves in Paris, yet living without display. I had occasion to remark that when those Roman princes were presented at the court of France they were only styled "marquis:" It was the same with the Russian princes, to whom the title of prince was refused when they wanted to be presented; they were called "knees," but they did not mind it, because that word meant prince. The court of France has always been foolishly particular on the question of titles, and is even now sparing of the title of monsieur, although it is common enough everywhere every man who was not titled was called Sieur. I have remarked that the king never addressed his bishops otherwise than as abbes, although they were generally very proud of their titles. The king likewise affected to know a nobleman only when his name was inscribed amongst those who served him.

Yet the haughtiness of Louis XV had been innoculated into him by education; it was not in his nature. When an ambassador presented someone to him, the person thus presented withdrew with the certainty of having been seen by the king, but that was all. Nevertheless, Louis XV was very polite, particularly with ladies, even with his mistresses, when in public. Whoever failed in respect towards them in the slightest manner was sure of disgrace, and no king ever possessed to a greater extent the grand royal virtue which is called dissimulation. He kept a secret faithfully, and he was delighted when he knew that no one but himself possessed it.

The Chevalier d'Eon is a proof of this, for the king alone knew and had always known that the chevalier was a woman, and all the long discussions which the false chevalier had with the office for foreign affairs was a comedy which the king allowed to go on, only because it amused him.

Louis XV was great in all things, and he would have had no faults if flattery had not forced them upon him. But how could he possibly have supposed himself faulty in anything when everyone around him repeated constantly that he was the best of kings? A king, in the opinion of which he was imbued respecting his own person, was a being of a nature by far too superior to ordinary men for him not to have the right to consider himself akin to a god. Sad destiny of kings! Vile flatterers are constantly doing everything necessary to reduce them below the condition of man.

The Princess of Ardore was delivered about that time of a young prince. Her husband, the Neapolitan ambassador, entreated Louis XV to be god-father to the child; the king consented and presented his god-son with a regiment; but the mother, who did not like the military career for her son, refused it. The Marshal de Richelieu told me that he had never known the king laugh so heartily as when he heard of that singular refusal.

At the Duchess de Fulvie's I made the acquaintance of Mdlle. Gaussin, who was called Lolotte. She was the mistress of Lord Albemarle, the English ambassador, a witty and very generous nobleman. One evening he complained of his mistress praising the beauty of the stars which were shining brightly over her head, saying that she ought to know he could not give them to her. If Lord Albemarle had been ambassador to the court of France at the time of the rupture between France and England, he would have arranged all difficulties amicably, and the unfortunate war by which France lost Canada would not have taken place. There is no doubt that the harmony between two nations depends very often upon their respective ambassadors, when there is any danger of a rupture.

As to the noble lord's mistress, there was but one opinion respecting her. She was fit in every way to become his wife, and the highest families of France did not think that she needed the title of Lady Albemarle to be received with distinction; no lady considered it debasing to sit near her, although she was well known as the mistress of the English lord. She had passed from her mother's arms to those of Lord Albemarle at the age of thirteen, and her conduct was always of the highest respectability. She bore children whom the ambassador acknowledged legally, and she died Countess d'Erouville. I shall have to mention her again in my Memoirs.

I had likewise occasion to become acquainted at the Venetian Embassy with a lady from Venice, the widow of an English baronet named Wynne. She was then coming from London with her children, where she had been compelled to go in order to insure them the inheritance of their late father, which they would have lost if they had not declared themselves members of the Church of England. She was on her way back to Venice, much pleased with her journey. She was accompanied by her eldest daughter—a young girl of twelve years, who, notwithstanding her youth, carried on her beautiful face all the signs of perfection.

She is now living in Venice, the widow of Count de Rosenberg, who died in Venice ambassador of the Empress-Queen Maria Theresa. She is surrounded by the brilliant halo of her excellent conduct and of all her social virtues. No one can accuse her of any fault, except that of being poor, but she feels it only because it does not allow her to be as charitable as she might wish.

The reader will see in the next chapter how I managed to embroil myself with the French police.

VIII

My Broil with Parisian Justice—Mdlle. Vesian.

The youngest daughter of my landlady, Mdlle. Quinson, a young girl between fifteen and sixteen years of age, was in the habit of often coming to my room without being called. It was not long before I discovered that she was in love with me, and I should have thought myself ridiculous if I had been cruel to a young brunette who was piquant, lively, amiable, and had a most delightful voice.

During the first four or five months nothing but childish trifles took place between us; but one night, coming home very late and finding her fast asleep on my bed, I did not see the necessity of waking her up, and undressing myself I lay down beside her. . . She left me at daybreak.

Mimi had not been gone three hours when a milliner came with a charming young girl, to invite herself and her friend to breakfast; I thought the young girl well worth a breakfast, but I was tired and wanted rest, and I begged them both to withdraw. Soon after they had left me, Madame Quinson came with her daughter to make my bed. I put my dressing-gown on, and began to write.

"Ah! the nasty hussies!" exclaims the mother.

"What is the matter, madam?"

"The riddle is clear enough, sir; these sheets are spoiled."

"I am very sorry, my dear madam, but change them, and the evil will be remedied at once."

She went out of the room, threatening and grumbling,

"Let them come again, and see if I don't take care of them!"

Mimi remained alone with me, and I addressed her some reproaches for her imprudence. But she laughed, and answered that Love had sent those women on purpose to protect Innocence! After that, Mimi was no longer under any restraint, she would come and share my bed whenever she had a fancy to do so, unless I sent her back to her own room, and in the morning she always left me in good time. But at the end of four months my beauty informed me that our secret would soon be discovered.

"I am very sorry," I said to her, "but I cannot help it."

"We ought to think of something."

"Well, do so."

"What can I think of? Well, come what will; the best thing I can do is not to think of it."

Towards the sixth month she had become so large, that her mother, no longer doubting the truth, got into a violent passion, and by dint of blows compelled her to name the father. Mimi said I was the guilty swain, and perhaps it was not an untruth.

With that great discovery Madame Quinson burst into my room in high dudgeon. She threw herself on a chair, and when she had recovered her breath she loaded me with insulting words, and ended by telling me that I must marry her daughter. At this intimation, understanding her object and wishing to cut the matter short, I told her that I was already married in Italy.

"Then why did you come here and get my daughter with child?"

"I can assure you that I did not mean to do so. Besides, how do you know that I am the father of the child?"

"Mimi says so, and she is certain of it."

"I congratulate her; but I warn you, madam, that I am ready to swear that I have not any certainty about it."

"What then?"

"Then nothing. If she is pregnant, she will be confined."

She went downstairs, uttering curses and threats: the next day I was summoned before the commissary of the district. I obeyed the summons, and found Madame Quinson fully equipped for the battle. The commissary, after the preliminary questions usual in all legal cases, asked me whether I admitted myself guilty towards the girl Quinson of the injury of which the mother, there present personally, complained.

"Monsieur le Commissaire, I beg of you to write word by word the answer which I am going to give you."

"Very well."

"I have caused no injury whatever to Mimi, the plaintiff's daughter, and I refer you to the girl herself, who has always had as much friendship for me as I have had for her."

"But she declares that she is pregnant from your doings."

"That may be, but it is not certain."

"She says it is certain, and she swears that she has never known any other man."

"If it is so, she is unfortunate; for in such a question a man cannot trust any woman but his own wife."

"What did you give her in order to seduce her?"

"Nothing; for very far from having seduced her, she has seduced me, and we agreed perfectly in one moment; a pretty woman does not find it very hard to seduce me."

"Was she a virgin?"

"I never felt any curiosity about it either before or after; therefore, sir, I do not know."

"Her mother claims reparation, and the law is against you."

"I can give no reparation to the mother; and as for the law I will obey it when it has been explained to me, and when I am convinced that I have been guilty against it."

"You are already convinced. Do you imagine that a man who gets an honest girl with child in a house of which he is an inmate does not transgress the laws of society?"

"I admit that to be the case when the mother is deceived; but when that same mother sends her daughter to the room of a young man, are we not right in supposing that she is disposed to accept peacefully all the accidents which may result from such conduct?"

"She sent her daughter to your room only to wait on you."

"And she has waited on me as I have waited on her if she sends her to my room this evening, and if it is agreeable to Mimi, I will certainly serve her as well as I can; but I will have nothing to do with her against her will or out of my room, the rent of which I have always paid punctually."

"You may say what you like, but you must pay the fine."

"I will say what I believe to be just, and I will pay nothing; for there can be no fine where there is no law transgressed. If I am sentenced to pay I shall appeal even to the last jurisdiction and until I obtain justice, for believe me, sir, I know that I am not such an awkward and cowardly fellow as to refuse my caresses to a pretty woman who pleases me, and comes to provoke them in my own room, especially when I feel myself certain of the mother's agreement."

I signed the interrogatory after I had read it carefully, and went away. The next day the lieutenant of police sent for me, and after he had heard me, as well as the mother and the daughter, he acquitted me and condemned Madame Quinson in costs. But I could not after all resist the tears of Mimi, and her entreaties for me to defray the expenses of her confinement. She was delivered of a boy, who was sent to the Hotel Dieu to be brought up at the nation's expense. Soon afterwards Mimi ran away from her mother's house, and she appeared on the stage at

St. Laurent's Fair. Being unknown, she had no difficulty in finding a lover who took her for a maiden. I found her very pretty on the stage.

"I did not know," I said to her, "that you were a musician."

"I am a musician about as much as all my companions, not one of whom knows a note of music. The girls at the opera are not much more clever, and in spite of that, with a good voice and some taste, one can sing delightfully."

I advised her to invite Patu to supper, and he was charmed with her. Some time afterwards, however, she came to a bad end, and disappeared.

The Italian comedians obtained at that time permission to perform parodies of operas and of tragedies. I made the acquaintance at that theatre of the celebrated Chantilly, who had been the mistress of the Marechal de Saxe, and was called Favart because the poet of that name had married her. She sang in the parody of 'Thetis et Pelee', by M. de Fontelle, the part of Tonton, amidst deafening applause. Her grace and talent won the love of a man of the greatest merit, the Abbe de Voisenon, with whom I was as intimate as with Crebillon. All the plays performed at the Italian Comedy, under the name of Madame Favart, were written by the abbe, who became member of the Academie after my departure from Paris. I cultivated an acquaintance the value of which I could appreciate, and he honoured me with his friendship. It was at my suggestions that the Abbe de Voisenon conceived the idea of composing oratorios in poetry; they were sung for the first time at the Tuileries, when the theatres were closed in consequence of some religious festival. That amiable abbe, who had written several comedies in secret, had very poor health and a very small body; he was all wit and gracefulness, famous for his shrewd repartees which, although very cutting, never offended anyone. It was impossible for him to have any enemies, for his criticism only grazed the skin and never wounded deeply. One day, as he was returning from Versailles, I asked him the news of the court.

"The king is yawning," he answered, "because he must come to the parliament to-morrow to hold a bed of justice."

"Why is it called a bed of justice?"

"I do not know, unless it is because justice is asleep during the proceedings."

I afterwards met in Prague the living portrait of that eminent writer in Count Francois Hardig, now plenipotentiary of the emperor at the court of Saxony.

The Abbe de Voisenon introduced me to Fontenelle, who was then ninety-three years of age. A fine wit, an amiable and learned man, celebrated for his quick repartees, Fontenelle could not pay a compliment without throwing kindness and wit into it. I told him that I had come from Italy on purpose to see him.

"Confess, sir," he said to me, "that you have kept me waiting a very long time."

This repartee was obliging and critical at the same time, and pointed out in a delicate and witty manner the untruth of my compliment. He made me a present of his works, and asked me if I liked the French plays; I told him that I had seen 'Thetis et Pelee' at the opera. That play was his own composition, and when I had praised it, he told me that it was a 'tete pelee'.

"I was at the Theatre Francais last night," I said, "and saw Athalie."

"It is the masterpiece of Racine; Voltaire, has been wrong in accusing me of having criticized that tragedy, and in attributing to me an epigram, the author of which has never been known, and which ends with two very poor lines:

> *"Pour avoir fait pis qu'Esther,*
> *Comment diable as-to pu faire"*

I have been told that M. de Fontenelle had been the tender friend of Madame du Tencin, that M. d'Alembert was the offspring of their intimacy, and that Le Rond had only been his foster-father. I knew d'Alembert at Madame de Graffigny's. That great philosopher had the talent of never appearing to be a learned man when he was in the company of amiable persons who had no pretension to learning or the sciences, and he always seemed to endow with intelligence those who conversed with him.

When I went to Paris for the second time, after my escape from The Leads of Venice, I was delighted at the idea of seeing again the amiable, venerable Fontenelle, but he died a fortnight after my arrival, at the beginning of the year 1757.

When I paid my third visit to Paris with the intention of ending my days in that capital, I reckoned upon the friendship of M. d'Alembert, but he died, like Fontenelle, a fortnight after my arrival, towards the end of 1783. Now I feel that I have seen Paris and France for the last time. The popular effervescence has disgusted me, and I am too old to hope to see the end of it.

Count de Looz, Polish ambassador at the French court, invited me in 1751 to translate into Italian a French opera susceptible of great transformations, and of having a grand ballet annexed to the subject of the opera itself. I chose 'Zoroastre', by M. de Cahusac. I had to adapt words to the music of the choruses, always a difficult task. The music remained very beautiful, of course, but my Italian poetry was very poor. In spite of that the generous sovereign sent me a splendid gold snuff-box, and I thus contrived at the same time to please my mother very highly.

It was about that time that Mdlle. Vesian arrived in Paris with her brother. She was quite young, well educated, beautiful, most amiable, and a novice; her brother accompanied her. Her father, formerly an officer in the French army, had died at Parma, his native city. Left an orphan without any means of support, she followed the advice given by her friends; she sold the furniture left by her father, with the intention of going to Versailles to obtain from the justice and from the generosity of the king a small pension to enable her to live. As she got out of the diligence, she took a coach, and desired to be taken to some hotel close by the Italian Theatre; by the greatest chance she was brought to the Hotel de Bourgogne, where I was then staying myself.

In the morning I was told that there were two young Italians, brother and sister, who did not appear very wealthy, in the next room to mine. Italians, young, poor and newly arrived, my curiosity was excited. I went to the door of their room, I knocked, and a young man came to open it in his shirt.

"I beg you to excuse me, sir," he said to me, "if I receive you in such a state."

"I have to ask your pardon myself. I only come to offer you my services, as a countryman and as a neighbour."

A mattress on the floor told me where the young man had slept; a bed standing in a recess and hid by curtains made me guess where the sister was. I begged of her to excuse me if I had presented myself without enquiring whether she was up.

She answered without seeing me, that the journey having greatly tried her she had slept a little later than usual, but that she would get up immediately if I would excuse her for a short time.

"I am going to my room, mademoiselle, and I will come back when you send for me; my room is next door to your own."

A quarter of an hour after, instead of being sent for, I saw a young and beautiful person enter my room; she made a modest bow, saying that she had come herself to return my visit, and that her brother would follow her immediately.

I thanked her for her visit, begged her to be seated, and I expressed all the interest I felt for her. Her gratitude shewed itself more by the tone of her voice than by her words, and her confidence being already captivated she told me artlessly, but not without some dignity, her short history or rather her situation, and she concluded by these words:

"I must in the course of the day find a less expensive lodging, for I only possess six francs."

I asked her whether she had any letters of recommendation, and she drew out of her pocket a parcel of papers containing seven or eight testimonials of good conduct and honesty, and a passport.

"Is this all you have, my dear countrywoman?"

"Yes. I intend to call with my brother upon the secretary of war, and I hope he will take pity on me."

"You do not know anybody here?"

"Not one person, sir; you are the first man in France to whom I have exposed my situation."

"I am a countryman of yours, and you are recommended to me by your position as well as by your age; I wish to be your adviser, if you will permit me."

"Ah, sir! how grateful I would be!"

"Do not mention it. Give me your papers, I will see what is to be done with them. Do not relate your history to anyone, and do not say one word about your position. You had better remain at this hotel. Here are two Louis which I will lend you until you are in a position to return them to me."

She accepted, expressing her heart-felt gratitude.

Mademoiselle Vesian was an interesting brunette of sixteen. She had a good knowledge of French and Italian, graceful manners, and a dignity which endowed her with a very noble appearance. She informed me of her affairs without meanness, yet without that timidity which seems to arise from a fear of the person who listens being disposed to take advantage of the distressing position confided to his honour. She seemed neither humiliated nor bold; she had hope, and she did not boast of her courage. Her virtue was by no means ostentatious, but there was in her an air of modesty which would certainly have put a restraint upon anyone disposed to fail in respect towards her. I felt the effect of it myself, for in spite of her beautiful eyes, her fine figure, of the freshness of her complexion, her transparent skin, her negligee—in one word, all that can tempt a man and which filled me with burning desires, I did not for one instant lose control over myself; she had inspired me with a feeling of respect which helped me to master my senses, and I promised myself not only to attempt nothing against her virtue, but also not to be the first man to make her deviate from the right path. I even thought it better to postpone to another interview a little speech on that subject, the result of which might be to make me follow a different course.

"You are now in a city," I said to her, "in which your destiny must unfold itself, and in which all the fine qualities which nature has so bountifully bestowed upon you, and which may ultimately cause your fortune, may likewise cause your ruin; for here, by dear countrywoman, wealthy men despise all libertine women except those who have offered them the sacrifice of their virtue. If you are virtuous, and are determined upon remaining so, prepare yourself to bear a great deal of misery; if you feel yourself sufficiently above what is called prejudice, if, in one word, you feel disposed to consent to everything, in order to secure a comfortable position, be very careful not to make a mistake. Distrust altogether the sweet words which every passionate man will address to you for the sake of obtaining your favours, for, his passion once satisfied, his ardour will cool down, and you will find yourself deceived. Be wary of your adorers; they will give you abundance of counterfeit coin, but do not trust them far. As far as I am concerned, I feel certain that I shall never injure you, and I hope to be of some use to you. To reassure you entirely on my account, I will treat you as if you were my sister, for I am too young to play the part of your father, and I would not tell you all this if I did not think you a very charming person."

Her brother joined us as we were talking together. He was a good-looking young man of eighteen, well made, but without any style about him; he spoke little, and his expression was devoid of individuality. We breakfasted together, and having asked him as we were at table for what profession he felt an inclination, he answered that he was disposed to do anything to earn an honourable living.

"Have you any peculiar talent?"

"I write pretty well."

"That is something. When you go out, mistrust everybody; do not enter any cafe, and never speak to anyone in the streets. Eat your meals in your room with your sister, and tell the landlady to give you a small closet to sleep in. Write something in French to-day, let me have it to-morrow morning, and we will see what can be done. As for you, mademoiselle, my books are at your disposal, I have your papers; tomorrow I may have some news to tell you; we shall not see each other again to-day, for I generally come home very late." She took a few books, made a modest reverence, and told me with a charming voice that she had every confidence in me.

Feeling disposed to be useful to her, wherever I went during that day I spoke of nothing but of her and of her affairs; and everywhere men and women told me that if she was pretty she could not fail, but that at all events it would be right for her to take all necessary steps. I received a promise that the brother should be employed in some office. I thought that the best plan would be to find some influential lady who would consent to present Mdlle. Vesian to M. d'Argenson, and I knew that in the mean time I could support her. I begged Silvia to mention the matter to Madame de Montconseil, who had very great influence with the secretary of war. She promised to do so, but she wished to be acquainted with the young girl.

I returned to the hotel towards eleven o'clock, and seeing that there was a light still burning in the room of Mdlle. Vesian I knocked at her door. She opened it, and told me that she had sat up in the hope of seeing me. I gave her an account of what I had done. I found her disposed to undertake all that was necessary, and most grateful for my assistance. She spoke of her position with an air of noble indifference which she assumed in order to restrain her tears; she succeeded in keeping them back, but the moisture in her eyes proved all the efforts she was making to prevent them from falling. We had talked for two hours, and going from one subject to another I learned that she had never loved, and that she was therefore worthy of a lover who would reward her in a proper manner for the sacrifice of her virtue. It would have been absurd to think that marriage was to be the reward of that sacrifice; the young girl had not yet made what is called a false step, but she had none of the prudish feelings of those girls who say that they would not take such a step for all the gold in the universe, and usually give way before the slightest attack; all my young friend wanted was to dispose of herself in a proper and advantageous manner.

I could not help sighing as I listened to her very sensible remarks, considering the position in which she was placed by an adverse destiny. Her sincerity was charming to me; I was burning with desire. Lucie of Pasean came back to my memory; I recollected how deeply I had repented the injury I had done in neglecting a sweet flower, which another man, and a less worthy one, had hastened to pluck; I felt myself near a lamb which would perhaps become the prey of some greedy wolf; and she, with her noble feelings, her careful education, and a candour which an impure breath would perhaps destroy for ever, was surely not destined for a lot of shame. I regretted I was not rich enough to make her fortune, and to save her honour and her virtue. I felt that I could neither make her mine in an illegitimate way nor be her guardian angel, and that by becoming her protector I should do her more harm than good; in one word, instead of helping her out of the unfortunate position in which she was, I should, perhaps, only contribute to her entire ruin. During that time I had her near me, speaking to her in a sentimental way, and not uttering one single word of love; but I kissed her hand and her arms too often without coming to a resolution, without beginning a thing which would have too rapidly come to an end, and which would have compelled me to keep her for myself; in that case, there would have been no longer any hope of a fortune for her, and for me no means of getting rid of her. I have loved women even to madness, but I have always loved liberty better; and whenever I have been in danger of losing it fate has come to my rescue.

I had remained about four hours with Mdlle. Vesian, consumed by the most intense desires, and I had had strength enough to conquer them. She could not attribute my reserve to a feeling of modesty, and not knowing why I did not shew more boldness she must have supposed that I was either ill or impotent. I left her, after inviting her to dinner for the next day.

We had a pleasant dinner, and her brother having gone out for a walk after our meal we looked together out of the window from which we could see all the carriages going to the Italian Comedy. I asked her whether she would like to go; she answered me with a smile of delight, and we started at once.

I placed her in the amphitheatre where I left her, telling her that we would meet at the hotel at eleven o'clock. I would not remain with her, in order to avoid the questions which would have been addressed to me, for the simpler her toilet was the more interesting she looked.

After I had left the theatre, I went to sup at Silvia's and returned to the hotel. I was surprised at the sight of an elegant carriage; I enquired to whom it belonged, and I was told that it was the carriage of a young nobleman who had supped with Mdlle. Vesian. She was getting on.

The first thing next morning, as I was putting my head out of the window, I saw a hackney coach stop at the door of the hotel; a young man, well dressed in a morning costume, came out of it, and a minute after I heard him enter the room of Mdlle. Vesian. Courage! I had made up my mind; I affected a feeling of complete indifference in order to deceive myself.

I dressed myself to go out, and while I was at my toilet Vesian came in and told me that he did not like to go into his sister's room because the gentleman who had supped with her had just arrived.

"That's a matter of course," I said.

"He is rich and very handsome. He wishes to take us himself to Versailles, and promises to procure some employment for me."

"I congratulate you. Who is he?"

"I do not know."

I placed in an envelope the papers she had entrusted to me, and I handed them to him to return to his sister. I then went out. When I came home towards three o'clock, the landlady gave me a letter which had been left for me by Mdlle. Vesian, who had left the hotel.

I went to my room, opened the letter, and read the following lines:

"I return the money you have lent me with my best thanks. The Count de Narbonne feels interested in me, and wishes to assist me and my brother. I shall inform you of everything, of the house in which he wishes me to go and live, where he promises to supply me all I want. Your friendship is very dear to me, and I entreat you not to forget me. My brother remains at the hotel, and my room belongs to me for the month. I have paid everything."

"Here is," said I to myself, "a second Lucie de Pasean, and I am a second time the dupe of my foolish delicacy, for I feel certain that the count will not make her happy. But I wash my hands of it all."

I went to the Theatre Francais in the evening, and enquired about Narbonne. The first person I spoke to told me,

"He is the son of a wealthy man, but a great libertine and up to his neck in debts."

Nice references, indeed! For a week I went to all the theatres and public places in the hope of making the acquaintance of the count, but I could not succeed, and I was beginning to forget the adventure when one morning, towards eight o'clock Vesian calling on me, told me that his sister was in her room and wished to speak to me. I followed him immediately. I found her looking unhappy and with eyes red from crying. She told her brother to go out for a walk, and when he had gone she spoke to me thus:

"M. de Narbonne, whom I thought an honest man, because I wanted him to be such, came to sit by me where you had left me at the theatre; he told me that my face had interested him, and he asked me who I was. I told him what I had told you. You had promised to think of me, but Narbonne told me that he did not want your assistance, as he could act by himself. I believed him, and I have been the dupe of my confidence in him; he has deceived me; he is a villain."

The tears were choking her: I went to the window so as to let her cry without restraint: a few minutes after, I came back and I sat down by her.

"Tell me all, my dear Vesian, unburden your heart freely, and do not think yourself guilty towards me; in reality I have been wrong more than you. Your heart would not now be a prey to sorrow if I had not been so imprudent as to leave you alone at the theatre."

"Alas, sir! do not say so; ought I to reproach you because you thought me so virtuous? Well, in a few words, the monster promised to shew me every care, every attention, on condition of my giving him an undeniable, proof of my affection and confidence—namely, to take a lodging without my brother in the house of a woman whom he represented as respectable. He insisted upon my brother not living with me, saying that evil-minded persons might suppose him to be my lover. I allowed myself to be persuaded. Unhappy creature! How could I give way without consulting you? He told me that the respectable woman to whom he would take me would accompany me to Versailles, and that he would send my brother there so that we should be both presented to the war secretary. After our first supper he told me that he would come and fetch me in a hackney coach the next morning. He presented me with two louis and a gold watch, and I thought I could accept those presents from a young nobleman who shewed so much interest in me. The woman to whom he introduced me did not seem to me as respectable as he had represented her to be. I have passed one week with her without his doing anything to benefit my position. He would come, go out, return as he pleased, telling me every day that it would be the morrow, and when the morrow came there was always some impediment. At last, at seven o'clock this morning, the woman told me that the count was obliged to go into the country, that a hackney coach would bring me back to his hotel, and that he would come and see me on his return. Then, affecting an air of sadness, she told me that I must give her back the watch because the count had forgotten to pay the watchmaker for it. I handed it to her immediately without saying a word, and wrapping the little I possessed in my handkerchief I came back here, where I arrived half an hour since."

"Do you hope to see him on his return from the country?"

"To see him again! Oh, Lord! why have I ever seen him?"

She was crying bitterly, and I must confess that no young girl ever moved me so deeply as she did by the expression of her grief. Pity replaced in my heart the tenderness I had felt for her a week before. The infamous proceedings of Narbonne disgusted me to that extent that, if I had known where to find him alone, I would immediately have compelled him to give me reparation. Of course, I took good care not to ask the poor girl to give me a detailed account of her stay in the house of Narbonne's respectable procurers; I could guess even more than I wanted to know, and to insist upon that recital would have humiliated Mdlle. Vesian. I could see all the infamy of the count in the taking back of the watch which belonged to her as a gift, and which the unhappy girl had earned but too well. I did all I could to dry her tears, and she begged me to be a father to her, assuring me that she would never again do anything to render her unworthy of my friendship, and that she would always be guided by my advice.

"Well, my dear young friend, what you must do now is not only to forget the unworthy count and his criminal conduct towards you, but also the fault of which you have been guilty. What is done cannot be undone, and the past is beyond remedy; but compose yourself, and recall the air of cheerfulness which shone on your countenance a week ago. Then I could read on your face honesty, candour, good faith, and the noble assurance which arouses sentiment in those who can appreciate its charm. You must let all those feelings shine again on your features; for they alone can interest honest people, and you require the general sympathy more than ever. My friendship is of little importance to you, but you may rely upon it all the more because I fancy that you have now a claim upon it which you had not a week ago: Be quite certain, I beg, that I will not abandon you until your position is properly settled. I cannot at present tell you more; but be sure that I will think of you."

"Ah, my friend! if you promise to think of me, I ask for no more. Oh! unhappy creature that I am; there is not a soul in the world who thinks of me."

She was: so deeply moved that she fainted away. I came to her assistance without calling anyone, and when she had recovered her consciousness and some calm, I told her a hundred stories, true or purely imaginary, of the knavish tricks played in Paris by men who think of nothing but of deceiving young girls. I told her a few amusing instances in order to make her more cheerful, and at last I told her that she ought to be thankful for what had happened to her with Narbonne, because that misfortune would give her prudence for the future.

During that long tete-a-tete I had no difficulty in abstaining from bestowing any caresses upon her; I did not even take her hand, for what I felt for her was a tender pity; and I was very happy when at the end of two hours I saw her calm and determined upon bearing misfortune like a heroine.

She suddenly rose from her seat, and, looking at me with an air of modest trustfulness, she said to me,

"Are, you particularly engaged in any way to-day?"

"No, my dear:"

"Well, then, be good enough to take me somewhere out of Paris; to some place where I can breathe the fresh air freely; I shall then recover that appearance which you think I must have to interest in my favour those who will see me; and if I can enjoy a quiet sleep throughout the next night I feel I shall be happy again."

"I am grateful to you for your confidence in me. We will go out as soon as I am dressed. Your brother will return in the mean time."

"Oh, never mind my brother!"

"His presence is, on the contrary, of great importance. Recollect, my dear Vesian, you must make Narbonne ashamed of his own conduct. You must consider that if he should happen to hear that, on the very day he abandoned you, you went into the country alone with me, he would triumph, and would certainly say that he has only treated you as you deserved. But if you go with your brother and me your countryman, you give no occasion for slander."

"I blush not to have made that remark myself. We will wait for my brother's return."

He was not long in coming back, and having sent for a coach we were on the point of going, when Baletti called on me. I introduced him to the young lady, and invited him to join our party. He accepted, and we started. As my only purpose was to amuse Mdlle. Vesian, I told the coachman to drive us to the Gros Caillou, where we made an excellent impromptu dinner, the cheerfulness of the guests making up for the deficiencies of the servants.

Vesian, feeling his head rather heavy, went out for a walk after dinner, and I remained alone with his sister and my friend Baletti. I observed with pleasure that Baletti thought her an agreeable girl, and it gave me the idea of asking him to teach her dancing. I informed him of her position, of the reason which had brought her to Paris, of the little hope there was of her obtaining a pension from the king, and of the necessity there was for her to do something to earn a living. Baletti answered that he would be happy to do anything, and when he had examined the figure and the general conformation of the young girl he said to her,

"I will get Lani to take you for the ballet at the opera."

"Then," I said, "you must begin your lessons tomorrow. Mdlle. Vesian stops at my hotel."

The young girl, full of wonder at my plan, began to laugh heartily, and said,

"But can an opera dancer be extemporized like a minister of state? I can dance the minuet, and my ear is good enough to enable me to go through a quadrille; but with the exception of that I cannot dance one step."

"Most of the ballet girls," said Baletti, "know no more than you do."

"And how much must I ask from M. Lani? I do not think I can expect much."

"Nothing. The ballet girls are not paid."

"Then where is the advantage for me?" she said, with a sigh; "how shall I live?"

"Do not think of that. Such as you are, you will soon find ten wealthy noblemen who will dispute amongst themselves for the honour of making up for the absence of salary. You have only to make a good choice, and I am certain that it will not be long before we see you covered with diamonds."

"Now I understand you. You suppose some great lord will keep me?"

"Precisely; and that will be much better than a pension of four hundred francs, which you would, perhaps, not obtain without making the same sacrifice."

Very much surprised, she looked at me to ascertain whether I was serious or only jesting.

Baletti having left us, I told her it was truly the best thing she could do, unless she preferred the sad position of waiting-maid to some grand lady.

"I would not be the 'femme de chambre' even of the queen."

"And 'figurante' at the opera?"

"Much rather."

"You are smiling?"

"Yes, for it is enough to make me laugh. I the mistress of a rich nobleman, who will cover me with diamonds! Well, I mean to choose the oldest."

"Quite right, my dear; only do not make him jealous."

"I promise you to be faithful to him. But shall he find a situation for my brother? However, until I am at the opera, until I have met with my elderly lover, who will give me the means to support myself?"

"I, my dear girl, my friend Baletti, and all my friends, without other interest than the pleasure of serving you, but with the hope that you will live quietly, and that we shall contribute to your happiness. Are you satisfied?"

"Quite so; I have promised myself to be guided entirely by your advice, and I entreat you to remain always my best friend."

We returned to Paris at night, I left Mdlle. Vesian at the hotel, and accompanied Baletti to his mother's. At supper-time, my friend begged Silvia to speak to M. Lani in favour of our 'protegee', Silvia said that it was a much better plan than to solicit a miserable pension which, perhaps, would not be granted. Then we talked of a project which was then spoken of, namely to sell all the appointments of ballet girls and of chorus singers at the opera. There was even some idea of asking a high price for them, for it was argued that the higher the price the more the girls would be esteemed. Such a project, in the midst of the scandalous habits and manners of the time, had a sort of apparent wisdom; for it would have ennobled in a way a class of women who with very few exceptions seem to glory in being contemptible.

There were, at that time at the opera, several figurantes, singers and dancers, ugly rather than plain, without any talent, who, in spite of it all, lived in great comfort; for it is admitted that at the opera a girl must needs renounce all modesty or starve. But if a girl, newly arrived there, is clever enough to remain virtuous only for one month, her fortune is certainly made, because then the noblemen enjoying a reputation of wisdom and virtue are the only ones who seek to get hold of her. Those men are delighted to hear their names mentioned in connection with the newly-arrived beauty; they even go so far as to allow her a few frolics, provided she takes pride in what they give her, and provided her infidelities are not too public. Besides, it is the fashion never to go to sup with one's mistress without giving her notice of the intended visit, and everyone must admit that it is a very wise custom.

I came back to the hotel towards eleven o'clock, and seeing that Mdlle. Vesian's room was still open I went in. She was in bed.

"Let me get up," she said, "for I want to speak to you."

"Do not disturb yourself; we can talk all the same, and I think you much prettier as you are."

"I am very glad of it."

"What have you got to tell me?"

"Nothing, except to speak of the profession I am going to adopt. I am going to practice virtue in order to find a man who loves it only to destroy it."

"Quite true; but almost everything is like that in this life. Man always refers everything to himself, and everyone is a tyrant in his own way. I am pleased to see you becoming a philosopher."

"How can one become a philosopher?"

"By thinking."

"Must one think a long while?"

"Throughout life."

"Then it is never over?"

"Never; but one improves as much as possible, and obtains the sum of happiness which one is susceptible of enjoying."

"And how can that happiness be felt?"

"By all the pleasure which the philosopher can procure when he is conscious of having obtained them by his own exertions, and especially by getting rid of the many prejudices which make of the majority of men a troop of grown-up children."

"What is pleasure? What is meant by prejudices?"

"Pleasure is the actual enjoyment of our senses; it is a complete satisfaction given to all our natural and sensual appetites; and, when our worn-out senses want repose, either to have breathing time, or to recover strength, pleasure comes from the imagination, which finds enjoyment in thinking of the happiness afforded by rest. The philosopher is a person who refuses no pleasures which do not produce greater sorrows, and who knows how to create new ones."

"And you say that it is done by getting rid of prejudices? Then tell me what prejudices are, and what must be done to get rid of them."

"Your question, my dear girl, is not an easy one to answer, for moral philosophy does not know a more important one, or a more difficult one to decide; it is a lesson which lasts throughout life. I will tell you in a few words that we call prejudice every so-called duty for the existence of which we find no reason in nature."

"Then nature must be the philosopher's principal study?"

"Indeed it is; the most learned of philosophers is the one who commits the fewest errors."

"What philosopher, in your opinion, has committed the smallest quantity of errors?"

"Socrates."

"Yet he was in error sometimes?"

"Yes, in metaphysics."

"Oh! never mind that, for I think he could very well manage without that study."

"You are mistaken; morals are only the metaphysics of physics; nature is everything, and I give you leave to consider as a madman whoever tells you that he has made a new discovery in metaphysics. But if I went on, my dear, I might appear rather obscure to you. Proceed slowly, think; let your maxims be the consequence of just reasoning, and keep your happiness in view; in the end you must be happy."

"I prefer the lesson you have just taught me to the one which M. Baletti will give me to-morrow; for I have an idea that it will weary me, and now I am much interested."

"How do you know that you are interested?"

"Because I wish you not to leave me."

"Truly, my dear Vesian, never has a philosopher described sympathy better than you have just done. How happy I feel! How is it that I wish to prove it by kissing you?"

"No doubt because, to be happy, the soul must agree with the senses."

"Indeed, my divine Vesian? Your intelligence is charming."

"It is your work, dear friend; and I am so grateful to you that I share your desires."

"What is there to prevent us from satisfying such natural desires? Let us embrace one another tenderly."

What a lesson in philosophy! It seemed to us such a sweet one, our happiness was so complete, that at daybreak we were still kissing one another, and it was only when we parted in the morning that we discovered that the door of the room had remained open all night.

Baletti gave her a few lessons, and she was received at the opera; but she did not remain there more than two or three months, regulating her conduct carefully according to the precepts I had laid out for her. She never received Narbonne again, and at last accepted a nobleman who proved himself very different from all others, for the first thing he did was to make her give up the stage, although it was not a thing according to the fashion of those days. I do not recollect his name exactly; it was Count of Tressan or Trean. She behaved in a respectable way, and remained with him until his death. No one speaks of her now, although she is living in very easy circumstances; but she is fifty-six, and in Paris a woman of that age is no longer considered as being among the living.

After she left the Hotel de Bourgogne, I never spoke to her. Whenever I met her covered with jewels and diamonds, our souls saluted each other with joy, but her happiness was too precious for me to make any attempt against it. Her brother found a situation, but I lost sight of him.

IX

The Beautiful O-Morphi—The Deceitful Painter—I
Practice Cabalism for the Duchess de Chartres
I Leave Paris—My Stay in Dresden and My Departure
from that City.

I went to St. Lawrence's Fair with my friend Patu, who, taking it into his head to sup with a Flemish actress known by the name of Morphi, invited me to go with him. I felt no inclination for the girl, but what can we refuse to a friend? I did as he wished. After we had supped with the actress, Patu fancied a night devoted to a more agreeable occupation, and as I did not want to leave him I asked for a sofa on which I could sleep quietly during the night.

Morphi had a sister, a slovenly girl of thirteen, who told me that if I would give her a crown she would abandon her bed to me. I agreed to her proposal, and she took me to a small closet where I found a straw palliasse on four pieces of wood.

"Do you call this a bed, my child?"

"I have no other, sir."

"Then I do not want it, and you shall not have the crown."

"Did you intend undressing yourself?"

"Of course."

"What an idea! There are no sheets."

"Do you sleep with your clothes on?"

"Oh, no!"

"Well, then, go to bed as usual, and you shall have the crown."

"Why?"

"I want to see you undressed."

"But you won't do anything to me?"

"Not the slightest thing."

She undressed, laid herself on her miserable straw bed, and covered herself with an old curtain. In that state, the impression made by her dirty tatters disappeared, and I only saw a perfect beauty. But I wanted to see her entirely. I tried to satisfy my wishes, she opposed some resistance, but a double crown of six francs made her obedient, and finding that her only fault was a complete absence of cleanliness, I began to wash her with my own hands.

You will allow me, dear reader, to suppose that you possess a simple and natural knowledge, namely, that admiration under such circumstances is inseparable from another kind of approbation; luckily, I found the young Morphi disposed to let me do all I pleased, except the only thing for which I did not care! She told me candidly that she would not allow me to do that one thing, because in her sister's estimation it was worth twenty-five louis. I answered that we would bargain on that capital point another time, but that we would not touch it for the present. Satisfied with what I said, all the rest was at my disposal, and I found in her a talent which had attained great perfection in spite of her precocity.

The young Helene faithfully handed to her sister the six francs I had given her, and she told her the way in which she had earned them. Before I left the house she told me that, as she was in want of money, she felt disposed to make some abatement on the price of twenty-five louis. I answered with a laugh that I would see her about it the next day. I related the whole affair to Patu, who accused me of exaggeration; and wishing to prove to him that I was a real connoisseur of female beauty I insisted upon his seeing Helene as I had seen her. He agreed with me that the chisel of Praxiteles had never carved anything more perfect. As white as a lily, Helene possessed all the beauties which nature and the art of the painter can possibly combine. The loveliness of her features was so heavenly that it carried to the soul an indefinable sentiment of ecstacy, a delightful calm. She was fair, but her beautiful blue eyes equalled the finest black eyes in brilliance.

I went to see her the next evening, and, not agreeing about the price, I made a bargain with her sister to give her twelve francs every time I paid her a visit, and it was agreed that we would occupy her room until I should make up my mind to pay six hundred francs. It was regular usury, but the Morphi came from a Greek race, and was above prejudices. I had no idea of giving such a large sum, because I felt no wish to obtain what it would have procured me; what I obtained was all I cared for.

The elder sister thought I was duped, for in two months I had paid three hundred francs without having done anything, and she attributed my reserve to avarice. Avarice, indeed! I took a fancy to possess a painting of that beautiful body, and a German artist painted it for me splendidly for six louis. The position in which he painted it was delightful. She was lying on her stomach, her arms and her bosom leaning on a pillow, and holding her head sideways as if she were partly on the back. The clever and tasteful artist had painted her nether parts with so much skill and truth that no one could have wished for anything more beautiful; I was delighted with that portrait; it was a speaking likeness, and I wrote under it, "O-Morphi," not a Homeric word, but a Greek one after all, and meaning beautiful.

But who can anticipate the wonderful and secret decrees of destiny! My friend Patu wished to have a copy of that portrait; one cannot refuse such a slight service to a friend, and I gave an order for it to the same painter. But the artist, having been summoned to Versailles, shewed that delightful painting with several others, and M. de St. Quentin found it so beautiful that he lost no time in shewing it the king. His Most Christian Majesty, a great connoisseur in that line, wished to ascertain with his own eyes if the artist had made a faithful copy; and in case the original should prove as beautiful as the copy, the son of St. Louis knew very well what to do with it.

M. de St. Quentin, the king's trusty friend, had the charge of that important affair; it was his province: He enquired from the painter whether the original could be brought to Versailles, and the artist, not supposing there would be any difficulty, promised to attend to it.

He therefore called on me to communicate the proposal; I thought it was delightful, and I immediately told the sister, who jumped for joy. She set to work cleaning, washing and clothing the young beauty, and two or three days after they went to Versailles with the painter to see what could be done. M. de St. Quentin's valet, having received his instructions from his master, took the two females to a pavilion in the park, and the painter went to the hotel to await the result of his negotiation. Half an hour afterwards the king entered the pavilion alone, asked the young O-Morphi if she was a Greek woman, took the portrait out of his pocket, and after a careful examination exclaimed,

"I have never seen a better likeness."

His majesty then sat down, took the young girl on his knees, bestowed a few caresses on her, and having ascertained with his royal hand that the fruit had not yet been plucked, he gave her a kiss.

O-Morphi was looking attentively at her master, and smiled.

"What are you laughing at?" said the king.

"I laugh because you and a crown of six francs are as like as two peas."

That naivete made the king laugh heartily, and he asked her whether she would like to remain in Versailles.

"That depends upon my sister," answered the child.

But the sister hastened to tell the king that she could not aspire to a greater honour. The king locked them up again in the pavilion and went away, but in less than a quarter of an hour St. Quentin came to fetch them, placed the young girl in an apartment under the care of a female attendant, and with the sister he went to meet at the hotel the German artist to whom he gave fifty Louis for the portrait, and nothing to Morphi. He only took her address, promising her that she would soon hear from him; the next day she received one thousand Louis. The worthy German gave me twenty-five louis for my portrait, with a promise to make a careful copy of the one I had given to Patu, and he offered to paint for me gratuitously the likeness of every girl of whom I might wish to keep a portrait.

I enjoyed heartily the pleasure of the good Fleeting, when she found herself in possession of the thousand gold pieces which she had received. Seeing herself rich, and considering me as the author of her fortune, she did not know how to shew me her gratitude.

The young and lovely O-Morphi—for the king always called her by that name—pleased the sovereign by her simplicity and her pretty ways more even than by her rare beauty—the most perfect, the most regular, I recollect to have ever seen. He placed her in one of the apartments of his Parc-dux-cerfs—the voluptuous monarch's harem, in which no one could get admittance except the ladies presented at the court. At the end of one year she gave birth to a son who went, like so many others, God knows where! for as long as Queen Mary lived no one ever knew what became of the natural children of Louis XV.

O-Morphi fell into disgrace at the end of three years, but the king, as he sent her away, ordered her to receive a sum of four hundred thousand francs which she brought as a dowry to an officer from Britanny. In 1783, happening to be in Fontainebleau, I made the acquaintance of a charming young man of twenty-five, the offspring of that marriage and the living portrait of his mother, of the history of whom he had not the slightest knowledge, and I thought it my duty not to enlighten him. I wrote my name on his tablets, and I begged him to present my compliments to his mother.

A wicked trick of Madame de Valentinois, sister-in-law of the Prince of Monaco, was the cause of O-Morphi's disgrace. That lady, who was well known in Paris, told her one day that, if she wished to make the king very merry, she had only to ask him how he treated his old wife. Too simple to guess the snare thus laid out for her, O-Morphi actually asked that impertinent question; but Louis XV gave her a look of fury, and exclaimed,

"Miserable wretch! who taught you to address me that question?"

The poor O-Morphi, almost dead with fright, threw herself on her knees, and confessed the truth.

The king left her and never would see her again. The Countess de Valentinois was exiled for two years from the court. Louis XV, who knew how wrongly he was behaving towards his wife as a husband, would not deserve any reproach at her hands as a king, and woe to anyone who forgot the respect due to the queen!

The French are undoubtedly the most witty people in Europe, and perhaps in the whole world, but Paris is, all the same, the city for impostors and quacks to make a fortune. When their knavery is found out people turn it into a joke and laugh, but in the midst of the merriment another mountebank makes his appearance, who does something more wonderful than those who preceded him, and he makes his fortune, whilst the scoffing of the people is in abeyance. It is the unquestionable effects of the power which fashion has over that amiable, clever, and lively nation. If anything is astonishing, no matter how extravagant it may be, the crowd is sure to welcome it greedily, for anyone would be afraid of being taken for a fool if he should exclaim, "It is impossible!" Physicians are, perhaps, the only men in France who know that an infinite gulf yawns between the will and the deed, whilst in Italy it is an axiom known to everybody; but I do not mean to say that the Italians are superior to the French.

A certain painter met with great success for some time by announcing a thing which was an impossibility—namely, by pretending that he could take a portrait of a person without seeing the individual, and only from the description given. But he wanted the description to be thoroughly accurate. The result of it was that the portrait did greater honour to the person who gave the description than—to the painter himself, but at the same time the informer found himself under the obligation of finding the likeness very good; otherwise the artist alleged the most legitimate excuse, and said that if the likeness was not perfect the fault was to be ascribed to the person who had given an imperfect description.

One evening I was taking supper at Silvia's when one of the guests spoke of that wonderful new artist, without laughing, and with every appearance of believing the whole affair.

"That painter," added he, "has already painted more than one hundred portraits, and they are all perfect likenesses."

Everybody was of the same opinion; it was splendid. I was the only one who, laughing heartily, took the liberty of saying it was absurd and impossible. The gentleman who had brought the wonderful news, feeling angry, proposed a wager of one hundred louis. I laughed all the more because his offer could not be accepted unless I exposed myself to being made a dupe.

"But the portraits are all admirable likenesses."

"I do not believe it, or if they are then there must be cheating somewhere."

But the gentleman, being bent upon convincing Silvia and me—for she had taken my part proposed to make us dine with the artist; and we accepted.

The next day we called upon the painter, where we saw a quantity of portraits, all of which the artist claimed to be speaking likenesses; as we did not know the persons whom they represented we could not deny his claim.

"Sir," said Silvia to the artist, "could you paint the likeness of my daughter without seeing her?"

"Yes, madam, if you are certain of giving me an exact description of the expression of her features."

We exchanged a glance, and no more was said about it. The painter told us that supper was his favourite meal, and that he would be delighted if we would often give him the pleasure of our company. Like all quacks, he possessed an immense quantity of letters and testimonials from Bordeaux, Toulouse, Lyons, Rouen, etc., which paid the highest compliments to the perfection of his portraits, or gave descriptions for new pictures ordered from him. His portraits, by the way, had to be paid for in advance.

Two or three days afterwards I met his pretty niece, who obligingly upbraided me for not having yet availed myself of her uncle's invitation to supper; the niece was a dainty morsel worthy of a king, and, her reproaches being very flattering to my vanity I promised I would come the next day. In less than a week it turned out a serious engagement. I fell in love with the interesting niece, who, being full of wit and well disposed to enjoy herself, had no love for me, and granted me no favour. I hoped, and, feeling that I was caught, I felt it was the only thing I could do.

One day that I was alone in my room, drinking my coffee and thinking of her, the door was suddenly opened without anyone being announced, and a young man came in. I did not recollect him, but, without giving me time to ask any questions, he said to me,

"Sir, I have had the honour of meeting you at the supper-table of M. Samson, the painter."

"Ah! yes; I beg you to excuse me, sir, I did not at first recollect you."

"It is natural, for your eyes are always on Mdlle. Samson."

"Very likely, but you must admit that she is a charming creature."

"I have no difficulty whatever in agreeing with you; to my misery, I know it but too well."

"You are in love with her?"

"Alas, yes! and I say, again, to my misery."

"To your misery? But why, do not you gain her love?"

"That is the very thing I have been striving for since last year, and I was beginning to have some hope when your arrival has reduced me to despair."

"I have reduced you to despair?"

"Yes, sir."

"I am very sorry, but I cannot help it."

"You could easily help it; and, if you would allow me, I could suggest to you the way in which you could greatly oblige me."

"Speak candidly."

"You might never put your foot in the house again."

"That is a rather singular proposal, but I agree that it is truly the only thing I can do if I have a real wish to oblige you. Do you think, however, that in that case you would succeed in gaining her affection?"

"Then it will be my business to succeed. Do not go there again, and I will take care of the rest."

"I might render you that very great service; but you must confess that you must have a singular opinion of me to suppose that I am a man to do such a thing."

"Yes, sir, I admit that it may appear singular; but I take you for a man of great sense and sound intellect, and after considering the subject deeply I have thought that you would put yourself in my place; that you would not wish to make me miserable, or to expose your own life for a young girl who can have inspired you with but a passing fancy, whilst my only wish is to secure the happiness or the misery of my life, whichever it may prove, by uniting her existence with mine."

"But suppose that I should intend, like you, to ask her in marriage?"

"Then we should both be worthy of pity, and one of us would have ceased to exist before the other obtained her, for as long as I shall live Mdlle. Samson shall not be the wife of another."

This young man, well-made, pale, grave, as cold as a piece of marble, madly in love, who, in his reason mixed with utter despair, came to speak to me in such a manner with the most surprising calm, made me pause and consider. Undoubtedly I was not afraid, but although in love with Mdlle. Samson I did not feel my passion sufficiently strong to cut the throat of a man for the sake of her beautiful eyes, or to lose my own life to defend my budding affection. Without answering the young man, I began to pace up and down my room, and for a quarter of an hour I weighed the following question which I put to myself: Which decision will appear more manly in the eyes of my rival and will win my own esteem to the deeper degree, namely-to accept coolly his offer to cut one another's throats, or to allay his anxiety by withdrawing from the field with dignity?

Pride whispered, Fight; Reason said, Compel thy rival to acknowledge thee a wiser man than he is.

"What would you think of me, sir," I said to him, with an air of decision, "if I consented to give up my visits to Mdlle. Samson?"

"I would think that you had pity on a miserable man, and I say that in that case you will ever find me ready to shed the last drop of my blood to prove my deep gratitude."

"Who are you?"

"My name is Garnier, I am the only son of M. Garnier, wine merchant in the Rue de Seine."

"Well, M. Garnier, I will never again call on Mdlle. Samson. Let us be friends."

"Until death. Farewell, sir."

"Adieu, be happy!"

Patu came in five minutes after Garnier had left me: I related the adventure to him, and he thought I was a hero.

"I would have acted as you have done," he observed, "but I would not have acted like Garnier."

It was about that time that the Count de Melfort, colonel of the Orleans regiment, entreated me through Camille, Coraline's sister, to answer two questions by means of my cabalism. I gave two answers very vague, yet meaning a great deal; I put them under a sealed envelope and gave them to Camille, who asked me the next day to accompany her to a place which she said she could not name to me. I followed her; she took me to the Palais-Royal, and then, through a narrow staircase, to the apartments of the Duchess de Chartres. I waited about a quarter of an hour, at the end of which time the duchess came in and loaded Camille with caresses for having brought me. Then addressing herself to me, she told me, with dignity yet very graciously, the difficulty she experienced in understanding the answers I had sent and which she was holding in her hand. At first I expressed some perplexity at the questions having emanated from her royal highness, and I told her afterwards that I understood cabalism, but that I could not interpret the meaning of the answers obtained through it, and that her highness must ask new questions likely to render the answers easier to be understood. She wrote down all she could not make out and all she wanted to know.

"Madam, you must be kind enough to divide the questions, for the cabalistic oracle never answers two questions at the same time."

"Well, then, prepare the questions yourself."

"Your highness will excuse me, but every word must be written with your own hand. Recollect, madam, that you will address yourself to a superior intelligence knowing all your secrets."

She began to write, and asked seven or eight questions. She read them over carefully, and said, with a face beaming with noble confidence,

"Sir, I wish to be certain that no one shall ever know what I have just written."

"Your highness may rely on my honour."

I read attentively, and I saw that her wish for secrecy was reasonable, and that if I put the questions in my pocket I should run the risk of losing them and implicating myself.

"I only require three hours to complete my task," I said to the duchess, "and I wish your highness to feel no anxiety. If you have any other engagement you can leave me here alone, provided I am not disturbed by anybody. When it is completed, I will put it all in a sealed envelope; I only want your highness to tell me to whom I must deliver the parcel."

"Either to me or to Madame de Polignac, if you know her."

"Yes, madam, I have the honour to know her."

The duchess handed me a small tinder-box to enable me to light a wax-candle, and she went away with Camille. I remained alone locked up in the room, and at the end of three hours, just as I had completed my task, Madame de Polignac came for the parcel and I left the palace.

The Duchess de Chartres, daughter of the Prince of Conti, was twenty-six years of age. She was endowed with that particular sort of wit which renders a woman adorable. She was lively, above the prejudices of rank, cheerful, full of jest, a lover of pleasure, which she preferred to a long life. "Short and sweet," were the words she had constantly on her lips. She was pretty but she stood badly, and used to laugh at Marcel, the teacher of graceful deportment, who wanted to correct her awkward bearing. She kept her head bent forward and her feet turned inside when dancing; yet she was a charming dancer. Unfortunately her face was covered with pimples, which injured her beauty very greatly. Her physicians thought that they were caused by a disease of the liver, but they came from impurity of the blood, which at last killed her, and from which she suffered throughout her life.

The questions she had asked from my oracle related to affairs connected with her heart, and she wished likewise to know how she could get rid of the blotches which disfigured her. My answers were rather obscure in such matters as I was not specially acquainted with, but they were very clear concerning her disease, and my oracle became precious and necessary to her highness.

The next day, after dinner, Camille wrote me a note, as I expected, requesting me to give up all other engagements in order to present myself at five o'clock at the Palais-Royal, in the same room in which the duchess had already received me the day before. I was punctual.

An elderly valet de chambre, who was waiting for me, immediately went to give notice of my arrival, and five minutes after the charming princess made her appearance. After addressing me in a very complimentary manner, she drew all my answers from her pocket, and enquired whether I had any pressing engagements.

"Your highness may be certain that I shall never have any more important business than to attend to your wishes."

"Very well; I do not intend to go out, and we can work."

She then shewed me all the questions which she had already prepared on different subjects, and particularly those relating to the cure of her pimples. One circumstance had contributed to render my oracle precious to her, because nobody could possibly know it, and I had guessed it. Had I not done so, I daresay it would have been all the same. I had laboured myself under the same disease, and I was enough of a physician to be aware that to attempt the cure of a cutaneous disease by active remedies might kill the patient.

I had already answered that she could not get rid of the pimples on her face in less than a week, but that a year of diet would be necessary to effect a radical cure.

We spent three hours in ascertaining what she was to do, and, believing implicitly in the power and in the science of the oracle, she undertook to follow faithfully everything ordered. Within one week all the ugly pimples had entirely disappeared.

I took care to purge her slightly; I prescribed every day what she was to eat, and forbade the use of all cosmetics; I only advised her to wash herself morning and evening with plantain water. The modest oracle told the princess to make use of the same water for her ablutions of every part of her body where she desired to obtain the same result, and she obeyed the prescription religiously.

I went to the opera on purpose on the day when the duchess shewed herself there with a smooth and rosy shin. After the opera, she took a walk in the great alley of the Palais-Royal, followed by the ladies of her suite and flattered by everybody. She saw me, and honoured me with a smile. I was truly happy. Camille, Madame de Polignac, and M. de Melfort were the only persons who knew that I was the oracle of the duchess, and I enjoyed my success. But the next day a few pimples reappeared on her beautiful complexion, and I received an order to repair at once to the Palais-Royal.

The valet, who did not know me, shewed me into a delightful boudoir near a closet in which there was a bath. The duchess came in; she looked sad, for she had several small pimples on the forehead and the chin. She held in her hand a question for the oracle, and as it was only a short one I thought it would give her the pleasure of finding the answer by herself. The numbers translated by the princess reproached her with having transgressed the regimen prescribed; she confessed to having drunk some liquors and eaten some ham; but she was astounded at having found that answer herself, and she could not understand how such an answer could result from an agglomeration of numbers. At that moment, one of her women came in to whisper a few words to her; she told her to wait outside, and turning towards me, she said,

"Have you any objection to seeing one of your friends who is as delicate as discreet?"

With these words, she hastily concealed in her pocket all the papers which did not relate to her disease; then she called out.

A man entered the room, whom I took for a stableboy; it was M. de Melfort.

"See," said the princess to him, "M. Casanova has taught me the cabalistic science."

And she shewed him the answer she had obtained herself. The count could not believe it.

"Well," said the duchess to me, "we must convince him. What shall I ask?"

"Anything your highness chooses."

She considered for one instant, and, drawing from her pocket a small ivory box, she wrote, "Tell me why this pomatum has no longer any effect."

She formed the pyramid, the columns, and the key, as I had taught her, and as she was ready to get the answer, I told her how to make the additions and subtractions which seem to come from the numbers, but which in reality are only arbitrary; then I told her to interpret the numbers in letters, and I left the room under some pretext. I came back when I thought that she had completed her translation, and I found her wrapped in amazement.

"Ah, sir!" she exclaimed, "what an answer!"

"Perhaps it is not the right one; but that will sometimes happen, madam."

"Not the right one, sir? It is divine! Here it is: That pomatum has no effect upon the skin of a woman who has been a mother."

"I do not see anything extraordinary in that answer, madam."

"Very likely, sir, but it is because you do not know that the pomatum in question was given to me five years ago by the Abbe de Brosses; it cured me at that time, but it was ten months before the birth of the Duke de Montpensier. I would give anything in the world to be thoroughly acquainted with that sublime cabalistic science."

"What!" said the count, "is it the pomatum the history of which I know?"

"Precisely."

"It is astonishing."

"I wish to ask one more question concerning a woman the name of whom I would rather not give."

"Say the woman whom I have in my thoughts."

She then asked this question: "What disease is that woman suffering from?" She made the calculation, and the answer which I made her bring forth was this: "She wants to deceive her husband." This time the duchess fairly screamed with astonishment.

It was getting very late, and I was preparing to take leave, when M. de Melfort, who was speaking to her highness, told me that we might go together. When we were out, he told me that the cabalistic answer concerning the pomatum was truly wonderful. This was the history of it:

"The duchess, pretty as you see her now, had her face so fearfully covered with pimples that the duke, thoroughly disgusted, had not the courage to come near her to enjoy his rights as a husband, and the poor princess was pining with useless longing to become a mother. The Abbe de Brosses cured her with that pomatum, and her beautiful face having entirely recovered it original bloom she made her appearance at the Theatre Francais, in the queen's box. The Duke de Chartres, not knowing that his wife had gone to the theatre, where she went but very seldom, was in the king's box. He did not recognize the duchess, but thinking her very handsome he enquired who she was, and when he was told he would not believe it; he left the royal box, went to his wife, complimented her, and announced his visit for the very same night. The result of that visit was, nine months afterwards, the birth of the Duke of Montpensier, who is now five years old and enjoys excellent health. During the whole of her pregnancy the duchess kept her face smooth and blooming, but immediately after her delivery the pimples reappeared, and the pomatum remained without any effect."

As he concluded his explanation, the count offered me a tortoise-shell box with a very good likeness of her royal highness, and said,

"The duchess begs your acceptance of this portrait, and, in case you would like to have it set she wishes you to make use of this for that purpose."

It was a purse of one hundred Louis. I accepted both, and entreated the count to offer the expressions of my profound gratitude to her highness. I never had the portrait mounted, for I was then in want of money for some other purpose.

After that, the duchess did me the honour of sending for me several times; but her cure remained altogether out of the question; she could not make up her mind to follow a regular diet. She would sometimes keep me at work for five or six hours, now in one corner, now in another, going in and out herself all the time, and having either dinner or supper brought to me by the old valet, who never uttered a word.

Her questions to the oracle alluded only to secret affairs which she was curious to know, and she often found truths with which I was not myself acquainted, through the answers. She wished me to teach her the cabalistic science, but she never pressed her wish upon me. She, however, commissioned M. de Melfort to tell me that, if I would teach her, she would get me an appointment with an income of twenty-five thousand francs. Alas! it was impossible! I was madly in love with her, but I would not for the world have allowed her to guess my feelings. My pride was the corrective of my love. I was afraid of her haughtiness humiliating me, and perhaps I was wrong. All I know is that I even now repent of having listened to a foolish pride. It is true that I enjoyed certain privileges which she might have refused me if she had known my love.

One day she wished my oracle to tell her whether it was possible to cure a cancer which Madame de la Popeliniere had in the breast; I took it in my head to answer that the lady alluded to had no cancer, and was enjoying excellent health.

"How is that?" said the duchess; "everyone in Paris believes her to be suffering from a cancer, and she has consultation upon consultation. Yet I have faith in the oracle."

Soon afterwards, seeing the Duke de Richelieu at the court, she told him she was certain that Madame de la Popeliniere was not ill. The marshal, who knew the secret, told her that she was mistaken; but she proposed a wager of a hundred thousand francs. I trembled when the duchess related the conversation to me.

"Has he accepted your wages?" I enquired, anxiously.

"No; he seemed surprised; you are aware that he ought to know the truth."

Three or four days after that conversation, the duchess told me triumphantly that M. de Richelieu had confessed to her that the cancer was only a ruse to excite the pity of her husband, with whom Madame de la Popeliniere wanted to live again on good terms; she added that the marshal had expressed his willingness to pay one thousand Louis to know how she had discovered the truth.

"If you wish to earn that sum," said the duchess to me, "I will tell him all about it."

But I was afraid of a snare; I knew the temper of the marshal, and the story of the hole in the wall through which he introduced himself into that lady's apartment, was the talk of all Paris. M. de la Popeliniere himself had made the adventure more public by refusing to live with his wife, to whom he paid an income of twelve thousand francs.

The Duchess de Chartres had written some charming poetry on that amusing affair; but out of her own coterie no one knew it except the king, who was fond of the princess, although she was in the habit of scoffing at him. One day, for instance, she asked him whether it was true that the king of Prussia was expected in Paris. Louis XV having answered that it was an idle rumour,

"I am very sorry," she said, "for I am longing to see a king."

My brother had completed several pictures and having decided on presenting one to M. de Marigny, we repaired one morning to the apartment of that nobleman, who lived in the Louvre, where all the artists were in the habit of paying their court to him. We were shewn into a hall adjoining his private apartment, and having arrived early we waited for M. de Marigny. My brother's picture was exposed there; it was a battle piece in the style of Bourguignon.

The first person who passed through the room stopped before the picture, examined it attentively, and moved on, evidently thinking that it was a poor painting; a moment afterwards two more persons came in, looked at the picture, smiled, and said,

"That's the work of a beginner."

I glanced at my brother, who was seated near me; he was in a fever. In less than a quarter of an hour the room was full of people, and the unfortunate picture was the butt of everybody's laughter. My poor brother felt almost dying, and thanked his stars that no one knew him personally.

The state of his mind was such that I heartily pitied him; I rose with the intention of going to some other room, and to console him I told him that M. de Marigny would soon come, and that his approbation of the picture would avenge him for the insults of the crowd. Fortunately, this was not my brother's opinion; we left the room hurriedly, took a coach, went home, and sent our servant to fetch back the painting. As soon as it had been brought back my brother made a battle of it in real earnest, for he cut it up with a sword into twenty pieces. He made up his mind to settle his affairs in Paris immediately, and to go somewhere else to study an art which he loved to idolatry; we resolved on going to Dresden together.

Two or three days before leaving the delightful city of Paris I dined alone at the house of the gate-keeper of the Tuileries; his name was

Conde. After dinner his wife, a rather pretty woman, presented me the bill, on which every item was reckoned at double its value. I pointed it out to her, but she answered very curtly that she could not abate one sou. I paid, and as the bill was receipted with the words 'femme Conde', I took the pen and to the word 'Conde' I added 'labre', and I went away leaving the bill on the table.

I was taking a walk in the Tuileries, not thinking any more of my female extortioner, when a small man, with his hat cocked on one side of his head and a large nosegay in his button-hole, and sporting a long sword, swaggered up to me and informed me, without any further explanation, that he had a fancy to cut my throat.

"But, my small specimen of humanity," I said, "you would require to jump on a chair to reach my throat. I will cut your ears."

"Sacre bleu, monsieur!"

"No vulgar passion, my dear sir; follow me; you shall soon be satisfied."

I walked rapidly towards the Porte de l'Etoile, where, seeing that the place was deserted, I abruptly asked the fellow what he wanted, and why he had attacked me.

"I am the Chevalier de Talvis," he answered. "You have insulted an honest woman who is under my protection; unsheath!"

With these words he drew his long sword; I unsheathed mine; after a minute or two I lunged rapidly, and wounded him in the breast. He jumped backward, exclaiming that I had wounded him treacherously.

"You lie, you rascally mannikin! acknowledge it, or I thrust my sword through your miserable body."

"You will not do it, for I am wounded; but I insist upon having my revenge, and we will leave the decision of this to competent judges."

"Miserable wrangler, wretched fighter, if you are not satisfied, I will cut off your ears!"

I left him there, satisfied that I had acted according to the laws of the duello, for he had drawn his sword before me, and if he had not been skilful enough to cover himself in good time, it was not, of course, my business to teach him. Towards the middle of August I left Paris with my brother. I had made a stay of two years in that city, the best in the world. I had enjoyed myself greatly, and had met with no unpleasantness except that I had been now and then short of money. We went through Metz, Mayence, and Frankfort, and arrived in Dresden at the end of the same month. My mother offered us the most affectionate welcome, and was delighted to see us again. My brother remained four years in that pleasant city, constantly engaged in the study of his art, and copying all the fine paintings of battles by the great masters in the celebrated Electoral Gallery.

He went back to Paris only when he felt certain that he could set criticism at defiance; I shall say hereafter how it was that we both reached that city about the same time. But before that period, dear, reader, you will see what good and adverse fortune did for or against me.

My life in Dresden until the end of the carnival in 1753 does not offer any extraordinary adventure. To please the actors, and especially my mother, I wrote a kind of melodrama, in which I brought out two harlequins. It was a parody of the 'Freres Ennemis', by Racine. The king was highly amused at the comic fancies which filled my play, and he made me a beautiful present. The king was grand and generous, and these qualities found a ready echo in the breast of the famous Count de Bruhl. I left Dresden soon after that, bidding adieu to my mother, to my brother Francois, and to my sister, then the wife of Pierre Auguste, chief player of the harpsichord at the Court, who died two years ago, leaving his widow and family in comfortable circumstances.

My stay in Dresden was marked by an amorous souvenir of which I got rid, as in previous similar circumstances, by a diet of six weeks. I have often remarked that the greatest part of my life was spent in trying to make myself ill, and when I had succeeded, in trying to recover my health. I have met with equal success in both things; and now that I enjoy excellent health in that line, I am very sorry to be physically unable to make myself ill again; but age, that cruel and unavoidable disease, compels me to be in good health in spite of myself. The illness I allude to, which the Italians call 'mal francais', although we might claim the honour of its first importation, does not shorten life, but it leaves indelible marks on the face. Those scars, less honourable perhaps than those which are won in the service of Mars, being obtained through pleasure, ought not to leave any regret behind.

In Dresden I had frequent opportunities of seeing the king, who was very fond of the Count de Bruhl, his minister, because that favourite possessed the double secret of shewing himself more extravagant even than his master, and of indulging all his whims.

Never was a monarch a greater enemy to economy; he laughed heartily when he was plundered and he spent a great deal in order to have occasion to laugh often. As he had not sufficient wit to amuse himself with the follies of other kings and with the absurdities of humankind, he kept four buffoons, who are called fools in Germany, although these degraded beings are generally more witty than their masters. The province of those jesters is to make their owner laugh by all sorts of jokes which are usually nothing but disgusting tricks, or low, impertinent jests.

Yet these professional buffoons sometimes captivate the mind of their master to such an extent that they obtain from him very important favours in behalf of the persons they protect, and the consequence is that they are often courted by the highest families. Where is the man who will not debase himself if he be in want? Does not Agamemnon say, in Homer, that in such a case man must necessarily be guilty of meanness? And Agamemnon and Homer lived long before our time! It evidently proves that men are at all times moved by the same motive- namely, self-interest.

It is wrong to say that the Count de Bruhl was the ruin of Saxony, for he was only the faithful minister of his royal master's inclinations. His children are poor, and justify their father's conduct.

The court at Dresden was at that time the most brilliant in Europe; the fine arts flourished, but there was no gallantry, for King Augustus had no inclination for the fair sex, and the Saxons were not of a nature to be thus inclined unless the example was set by their sovereign.

At my arrival in Prague, where I did not intend to stop, I delivered a letter I had for Locatelli, manager of the opera, and went to pay a visit to Madame Morelli, an old acquaintance, for whom I had great affection, and for two or three days she supplied all the wants of my heart.

As I was on the point of leaving Prague, I met in the street my friend Fabris, who had become a colonel, and he insisted upon my dining with him. After 'embracing him, I represented to him, but in vain, that I had made all my arrangements to go away immediately.

"You will go this evening," he said, "with a friend of mine, and you will catch the coach."

I had to give way, and I was delighted to have done so, for the remainder of the day passed in the most agreeable manner. Fabris was longing for war, and his wishes were gratified two years afterwards; he covered himself with glory.

I must say one word about Locatelli, who was an original character well worthy to be known. He took his meals every day at a table laid out for thirty persons, and the guests were his actors, actresses, dancers of both sexes, and a few friends. He did the honours of his well-supplied board nobly, and his real passion was good living. I shall have occasion to mention him again at the time of my journey to St. Petersburg, where I met him, and where he died only lately at the age of ninety.

A Note About the Author

Giacomo Casanova (1725–1798) was an Italian adventurer and author. Born in Venice, Casanova was the eldest of six siblings born to Gaetano Casanova and Zanetta Farussi, an actor and actress. Raised in a city noted for its cosmopolitanism, night life, and glamor, Casanova overcame a sickly childhood to excel in school, entering the University of Padua at the age of 12. After graduating in 1742 with a degree in law, he struggled to balance his work as a lawyer and low-level cleric with a growing gambling addiction. As scandals and a prison sentence threatened to derail his career in the church, Casanova managed to find work as a scribe for a powerful Cardinal in Rome, but was soon dismissed and entered military service for the Republic of Venice. Over the next several years, he left the service, succeeded as a professional gambler, and embarked on a Grand Tour of Europe. Towards the end of his life, Casanova worked on his exhaustive, scandalous memoirs, a 12-volume autobiography reflecting on a legendary life of romance and debauchery that brought him from the heights of aristocratic society to the lows of illness and imprisonment. Recognized for his self-styled sensationalism as much as he is for his detailed chronicling of 18th century European culture, Casanova is a man whose name is now synonymous with the kind of life he led—fast, fearless, and free.

A Note from the Publisher

Spanning many genres, from non-fiction essays to literature classics to children's books and lyric poetry, Mint Edition books showcase the master works of our time in a modern new package. The text is freshly typeset, is clean and easy to read, and features a new note about the author in each volume. Many books also include exclusive new introductory material. Every book boasts a striking new cover, which makes it as appropriate for collecting as it is for gift giving. Mint Edition books are only printed when a reader orders them, so natural resources are not wasted. We're proud that our books are never manufactured in excess and exist only in the exact quantity they need to be read and enjoyed.

Discover more of your favorite classics with Bookfinity™.

- Track your reading with custom book lists.
- Get great book recommendations for your personalized Reader Type.
- Add reviews for your favorite books.
- AND MUCH MORE!

Visit **bookfinity.com** and take the fun Reader Type quiz to get started.

Enjoy our classic and modern companion pairings!

Bookfinity is a registered trademark of Ingram Book Group LLC. © 2023 Bookfinity. All rights reserved.

www.ingramcontent.com/pod-product-compliance
Lightning Source LLC
Chambersburg PA
CBHW031445040426
42444CB00007B/985